Library of Congress Number: 98-073771

ISBN 1-56044-674-9

Manufactured in Korea
First Edition/Fourth Printing

The Globe Pequot Press

www.globe-pequot.com

Doyle River Falls, Shenandoah National Park WILLARD CLAY

introduction

The Mona Lisa of America, Virginia teases us out of mind with a slight smile and air of gentle, dreamy repose. For years it had the reputation of being the most conservative of states, but behind that placid exterior swift changes have been occurring. In the 1960s it lifted barriers to voting and enlarged funds for human services. In 1970 its people ratified progressive changes when a half dozen other states were rejecting revisions of their constitutions. An influx of newcomers in the 1980s made Virginia in 1990 the sixth-fastest growing state, with nearly two-thirds of a population of six million residing in the urban crescent from northern Virginia to Hampton Roads.

Yet its people may draw upon a past in which Virginians led the struggle for independence and then supplied four of the first five presidents in framing the new government. They feel it has the capability of blending the best of the past with the demands of the future. And much of its heritage, natural and historic, abides.

The white tundra swan returns in September to the blue waters around Assateague Island off Virginia's Eastern Shore, setting back its giant wings like nylon chutes, thrusting out its black-webbed feet as buoys just before it touches down and settles on the water so softly not a feather is mussed, then furling its white wings as gracefully as a ballerina taking a bow.... Along Virginia Beach the whitecaps march, row on row, against the shore in the ceaseless war between surf and sand. Back of the beach in Seashore State Park, Spanish moss drapes the trees, greybeards, old soldiers reflecting over dark pools.... And in the midst of the million-strong metropolis of Hampton Roads, 375 black bears roam 106,000 acres of the Dismal Swamp Refuge spreading across portions of the cities of Chesapeake and Portsmouth and three North Carolina counties.

The storied James River, having journeyed from the mountains through the piedmont, tumbles across the rocks under Richmond's ramparts and winds in jumprope loops across the alluvial plain of Hampton Roads, reluctant to leave the land now, doubling on itself to look back where it has been, a Virginia river to the end.... The Blue Ridge Mountains, through a trick of the atmosphere, appear under the afternoon sun as a veil that might be parted with a hand. Between the Blue Ridge and the Alleghenies runs the Great Valley along which pioneers moved westward. In the fall, Virginians make a pilgrimage there, marveling at the mountainsides aflame with foliage of red, orange, bronze, and yellow as if thronged with jostling Indians in war paint and feathers descending to reclaim their lands, while ahead of them scrub pines crouch on the Valley floor, reconnoitering scouts, amid the broom straw....

Virginia's mountains, worn down by time, are a grandfatherly lot. The Skyline Drive wriggles 105 miles along the top of the Blue Ridge Parkway through 194,000 acres of Shenandoah National Park, which claims sixty peaks between three thousand and four thousand feet high. Near Bedford are the Peaks of Otter, Flat Top, and Sharp Top. With a coxcomb crest of boulders, Sharp Top seems a rostrum from which to address the universe. John Randolph of Roanoke was so moved by the view he commanded his servant to join him in prayer. At Afton, Skyline Drive changes to Blue Ridge Parkway and continues 217 miles into North Carolina. Once a sea lapped at the Blue Ridge's western slopes. When the hills hump their backs through morning mists, the waters seem to have come again, with whales.

In southwest Virginia is Mount Rogers, a vast mountain tableland once crowned with prime spruce and fir. At the century's turn, lumber companies began building railroads into the high country, bought timber rights from the mountaineers for a new shotgun, cut thousands of acres, then set fire to the slash and debris. The flames, seen for miles writhing on the mountain, cracked rock pinnacles. The plateau in the sky came back in grassland. Lavender mountain laurel and purple rhododendron run riot amid gray house-sized boulders in the spring. The air is hushed and clean, and it is worth a trip just to breathe it.

It was here, on the slopes of Mount Rogers, I visited Catherine Blevins, berry picking near her cabin above a creek. Catherine churned butter and sent it to town at fifty cents a pound, which brought $68 to feed the cow and the hog, she said, as if that was as much as anybody had a right to expect, a balancing of the books with nature. Her eyes were as blue as the sky reflected in the mountain spring, and as untroubled; her face, untouched by cosmetics, was ruddy as a fall apple, lovely under a crown of white hair pulled back into a knot and streaked yellow with the sun.

Catherine visited her seven children (and twenty-four great-grandchildren), but insisted on staying with the cabin. From her garden she gathered and canned vegetables and fruits. In the morning, she built a fire in the wood cookstove and went to turn in the cow with the calf and fed the pig and came back to get her breakfast and went back and milked the cow after the calf got through. So she went until night fell on the mountain, a slow, soft blanket. She was at one

A ruby-throated hummingbird enjoying nectar from a Mexican sunflower   JOHN M. COFFMAN

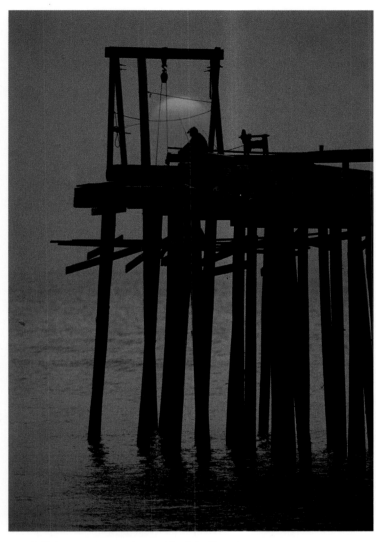

A fisherman's sunrise at Virginia Beach RAYMOND GEHMAN

with the seasons, as deliberate and steady as their turning. The sweetness and integrity of her life is replicated by the watermen on the coast.

Such as Tom Reed, a "munger," (one who makes a living from the marsh and the sea), who became a valued assistant with federal wildlife research teams. His face is as tan and unlined as hard-packed sand. He is as sturdy as the wild ponies that are rounded up each July for sale to support the volunteer fire department in Chincoteague. He fits Jefferson's vision of a man at one with nature and work. His voice is the sort a person would expect to hear when putting a seashell to the ear, with a forthright sounding of the vowel "o" so that the pronoun "I" becomes full-bodied "Oy" and time becomes "toime." To dig clams, he wore a blue flannel shirt, oilskin coat, and linen moccasins. "You'd curl your foot around a clam, with a dab of mud and then—quick!—with the pressure of the water and the mud, you'd rake it up. 'Leggin' 'em,' we called it. When the water's deeper, you hold the clam between your feet, bear your weight on the boat, and you jump and catch 'em. It was hard. A lot of toimes I dreaded to go in the cold, but it was a rewarding loif, it seems to me loike, and I believe if I had to live my loif over again, I'd loike to do the same thing."

Virginia cityscapes excite, too. Set amid Richmond's skyscrapers is Capital Square, a green hill topped by the columned, oyster-gray Statehouse designed by Thomas Jefferson. Centered in the Rotunda between the House and Senate of the General Assembly is a statue beyond compare, the life-size marble likeness of George Washington, done from life by Jean Houdon. Wearing his old military coat from which two buttons were missing, Washington was 53, done with war but not yet elected to the presidency. Houdon worked two weeks trying to get just the right expression on Washington's face. Along came a mule trader to Mount Vernon and when the trader mentioned a price, Washington's mouth tightened—and Houdon had him. Between the two chambers, legislators pause to trade beneath Father Washington's severe and steady stare.

In Hampton Roads, on the horizons of Norfolk, Portsmouth, and Newport News, loom sixteen-story, orange-limbed Martian monsters: double-hoist cranes that keep Virginia ports competitive as the fastest-growing, fastest-working piers on the East Coast. Newport News ports connect with CSX trains and Norfolk's piers tie in with the Norfolk Southern Railway. In Roanoke are the world's finest railroad shops. Occasionally, they fire up one of the old mighty steam locomotives for an excursion. When the locomotive whistles, the steam gives its voice a hoarse, haunting, living quality, and people in Big Lick lift their heads and smile at the sound.

Anchoring Hampton Roads' sprawling military complex is the Norfolk Naval Base, offering the moving spectacle of families waiting on the pier to welcome five thousand men standing at attention around the flight deck of a huge carrier, the ship nosing around the river's bend and slowly halting like an immense mesa beside the multitude. You can feel the tides of passion as those on deck and dock strain to pick loved ones out of the masses. Then the sailors come pounding like rapids down the gangplanks until, in a whirlpool of emotions, families are whole again waltzing in each other's arms, pounding backs, crying, laughing. The pier empties gradually as they leave arm-in-arm, children riding their father's shoulders, receding to homes across the country while the great ship sits quietly, waiting.

Despite television's leveling effect, Virginians' accents persist. Let a Virginian listen, blindfolded, to talk anywhere in the state and he or she can identify the place. If a visiting Englishman encountered the broad "a," still passed around like a cup of tea (or glass of sherry) among members of some of the old families of Richmond and upper Tidewater, he might conclude he was on the Thames instead of the James. In the classic accent prevalent in Richmond, plain "house" becomes "how-oos." Ordinary "out" becomes "ow-oot" and "about" is transformed into "abaa-oot." You will recognize them when you hear them, as I did once during a high school performance of "Macbeth." When Lady Macbeth strayed on stage, sleep-walking, washing her hands, she intoned: "Ow-oo-ut, ow-oo-ut, da-yum spah-woot!"—as if she were turning a naughty dog into the night. Occasionally, still, you hear a Virginian insert a "y" into a word, so that "garden" becomes "gahden" and "car" is "cyah." It makes life seem ever so much finer, somehow.

In southwest Virginia, a teacher told her pupils the Christmas story about the three wise men arriving from afar to offer gifts to the babe in the manger. She asked her fourth-graders to come dressed next day in Christmas costumes. One boy, whose father was a volunteer fireman, came wearing a magnificent red fireman's helmet. But what, the teacher asked the child, did a fireman's hat have to do with the Christmas story?

"Didn't you tell us that the three wise men come from a far?" the boy replied.

The Old Dominion's reputation for hospitality traces to colonial times when Virginians thirsted for word from the outside world. They would seize a stranger and hold him or her enthralled for days like Circe charmed and penned the sailors of Odysseus. All a traveler had to do was inquire upon the road where any gentleman lived, and he could count on being welcomed. Visitors left accounts as if Virginians were a fabulous race of the sort Gulliver found. "Almost every person keeps a horse," marveled one, "and I have known some spending the morning ranging several miles in the woods to find and catch their horses to ride two or three miles to Church, to the Court House, or to a Horse Race."

Visiting still is a prime amusement, evident in the reluctance of two Virginia women to part after a long talk. They will be on the verge, at last, of saying goodbye, their husbands stirring into life by the cars on which they have been leaning, when suddenly one woman, in the act of putting her foot in the car to depart, will say, "Oh, by the way, I heard the other day from Betsy Lou!" Off they go on another round of conversation. The men lapse again against the cars.

Festivals flourish in Virginia from April to October. These convivial gatherings feature oysters, country ham (long cure and short), barbecued beef, pork, and chicken, baked shad, maple syrup, apple butter, shrimp, crabs, peaches, peanuts.... One could live nine months a year simply by attending each day's groaning board.

Nearly every step one takes here is on hallowed ground. Two-thirds of the battles of the Civil War—that dark "Hamlet" of the American soul, Bruce Catton called it—were fought in Virginia. To grasp the tragedy, view any battlefield. At Cold Harbor on June 3, 1864, General Grant threw sixty thousand troops, half his army, against Lee's entrenched men. The night before, the Federal soldiers had heard the Confederates digging in. Grant's men knew they would face death and many pinned their names and addresses to their coats before they went into battle. The assault lasted eight minutes—and eight thousand Union soldiers fell.

Go, for the nation's beginning, to Jamestown. There in 1607, 105 settlers disembarked from three tiny ships to undertake the first English settlement in the New World, nineteen years before the Pilgrims touched Plymouth Rock. Now and then a tourist marches into the Jamestown museum and asks, "Where is the rock?" The colony survived thanks to a stocky soldier, Captain John Smith, and an Indian teenager, Pocahontas, daughter of Emperor Powhatan. "He that will not worke will not eat," Smith declared, and he would pour a dipper of cold water down a layabout's sleeve. Pocahontas slipped through the woods to warn the settlers of impending Indian raids. That child of a Stone Age civilization visited and charmed the Court of St. James' in London. As she lay dying, her last words were to her sorrowing husband, settler John Rolfe, about their son. "What does it matter so long as the child liveth?" she asked. He thrived, as did the colony she had saved. "The mother of us all," poet Vachel Lindsay called her.

After fires and malaria beset Jamestown, the settlers moved to higher ground at Williamsburg, which became the training ground for statesmen. There Thomas Jefferson whetted his intellect. Patrick Henry cried treason against the British crown. George Washington put on his uniform for the French and Indian Wars and honed the skills he turned against the British in the American Revolution. John Marshall learned law from George Wythe. A few miles away at Yorktown, on a bluff overlooking the York River, lies the battlefield where Washington, with the aid of the French, trapped General Cornwallis and his Redcoats in 1781 and won American independence. In the visitors center is his headquarter's tent. For eight years Americans' hopes for freedom were pinned on that patch of canvas. Didn't make any difference how many battles the Americans lost, a French observer reported to his king. In the end they would win the war because they had Washington. At the Battle of Monmouth, his troops in a rout, Washington appeared on his white charger, as if dropped from the sky, to rally them. A major covered his eyes, fearful he might see Washington fall in the hail of bullets. The war ended, all Washington wanted was to farm Mount Vernon. The American people had other ideas.

Near Mount Vernon on the Potomac River is Gunston Hall, the elegant little mansion of

Yellow buds of an early-blooming crocus breaking through a lingering snowbank WILLIAM B. FOLSOM

George Mason, who was always reluctant to leave it. Inside is the table on which he wrote Virginia's Declaration of Rights, which became the basis of the nation's Bill of Rights. Mason, a leader in framing the U.S. Constitution, refused to sign it when the convention recognized slavery and failed to include a Bill of Rights. James Madison, who lived at Montpelier, near Jefferson's Monticello, saw that the first amendments to the Constitution included the Bill of Rights. In Richmond is the home of John Marshall, the fourth and great Chief Justice who made the U.S. Supreme Court supreme with his finding that the Court had the power to review the constitutionality of the acts of Congress. "I went in the army a Virginian, and I came out an American," Marshall said. He died in Philadelphia. As his body was borne to the ship that would take it home, the Liberty Bell tolled, and it was then that it cracked.

Stratford Hall in Westmoreland County was the home of the five Lee brothers who served their country during the Revolution. Both Richard Henry Lee and Francis Lightfoot Lee signed the Declaration of Independence. A sixth brother, a Tory, sat out the war on the sidelines. The Lees formed an axis with John Adams of Massachusetts who called them, "A band of brothers, intrepid and unchangeable..." who stood in the gap like the Greeks at Thermopylae.

As Washington led the fighting, Thomas Jefferson did the writing of newly won rights into the Virginia law. "Our Revolution," he wrote later, "presented us with an album on which we could write what we pleased." Jefferson would be astonished at the splendid condition of Monticello, his home near Charlottesville. As with many patriots who pledged their lives, fortunes, and sacred honor to achieve freedom, Jefferson died broke. But the cannonball clock is still rigged over Monticello's entrance. His other labor-saving devices—dumbwaiter, revolving bookcase, duplicator of correspondence—are in readiness. He'd be elated that the University of

Virginia, which he founded as the "bantling" of his old age, is flourishing. In a 1976 poll of American architects, a majority choose as the nation's "proudest achievement" in architecture the University's green lawn between the two long rows of two-story pavilions headed by the towering Rotunda. The vast sunlit expanse under the Rotunda's domed skylight is often termed America's most beautiful room.

Jefferson failed in efforts to abolish slavery, but he was able to exclude it from the Northwest Territory. He and the other founders left tools with which to continue their works. In Virginia two strands contend in creative tension. One hearkens to the past, clinging to what we know and cherish. The other, receiving a powerful thrust from Jefferson, looks to the future and things as they might better be. "I steer my bark with Hope in the head, leaving fears astern," Jefferson wrote John Adams.

Declining to join the citizens in Washington, D.C., in celebrating the fiftieth anniversary of the Declaration of Independence, Jefferson wrote on June 24, 1826: "All our eyes are opened, or opening, to the right of man. The general spread of the light of science has already laid open to every view the palpable truth, that the mass of mankind has not been born with saddles on their backs, nor a favored few booted and spurred, ready to ride them legitimately, by the grace by God. There are grounds of Hope for others. For ourselves let the annual return of this day forever refresh our recollections of these rights, and an undiminished devotion to them...."

On that Fourth of July both Jefferson and Adams died. Not knowing that his Virginia friend had preceded him in death by a little time, Adams said in his dying words: "Thomas Jefferson lives."

As do all the great patriots.

Guy Friddell
Norfolk

A whitetail doe standing backlit by the golden haze of sunrise, Albemarle County   JAMES FRANK

A kaleidoscopic display of azaleas   MAE SCANLAN

" You found at every twist of the road another patch of blossoms—purple and lavender bowers of flowers clinging to the mountainsides, held high to the sun, explosions of color—like... peering as a child into your first kaleidoscope and thinking the next turn couldn't possibly be different and being surprised anew by the flaming combinations. "

Guy Friddell,
We Began at Jamestown

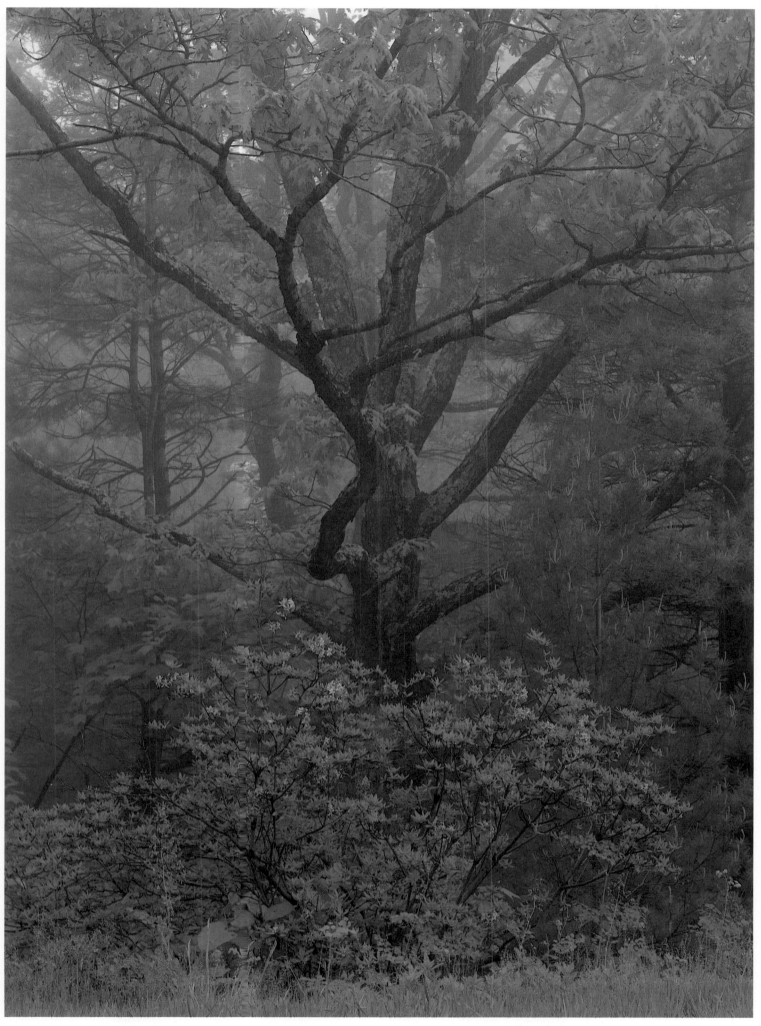

Fog-shrouded symbols of Virginia—a tall oak and wild azalea in the Blue Ridge Mountains   WILLARD CLAY

❝ *Heaven and earth never agreed better to frame a place for man's habitation. Here are hills, plains, valleys, rivers and brooks, all running most pleasantly into a faire bay encompassed about with fruitful and delightsome land.* **❞**

Captain John Smith

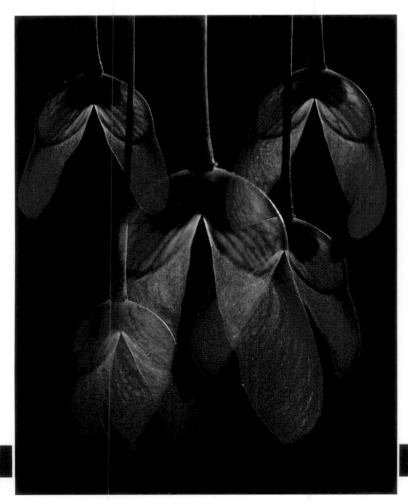

Maple seeds   JOHN M. COFFMAN

Red-leaved sweetgum and green-needled loblolly pine competing for attention in Seashore State Park, near Virginia Beach   CARR CLIFTON

" *The benign, smiling Blue Ridge… has a trick of almost fading away into nothingness, becoming part and parcel of the azure air, atomizing before your very eyes, a wispy, lightly-patterned veil rather than a wall, as if you could see through its mountains, much like those into which the Pied Piper disappeared.* **"**

Guy Friddell,
What Is It about Virginia?

The benign Blue Ridge Mountains from McAfee's Knob near Roanoke   FRED CRAMER

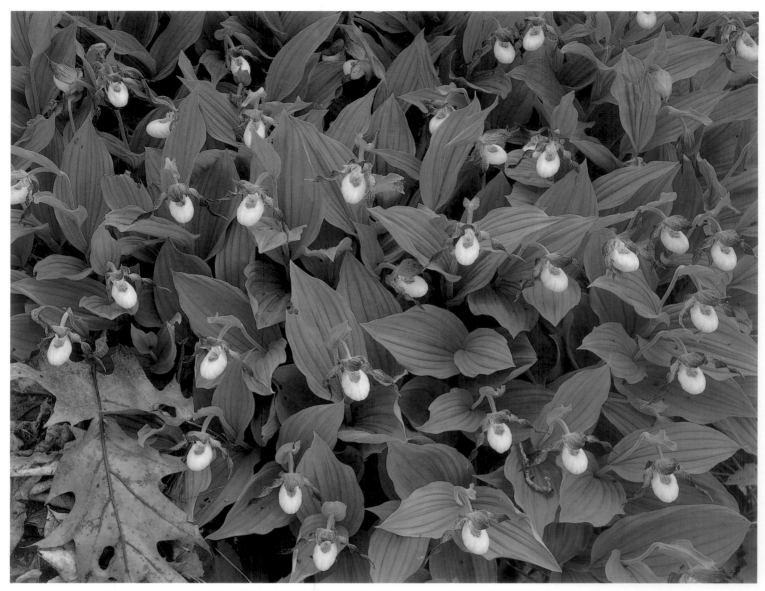

A dense patch of yellow lady's slippers, some of Virginia's loveliest wild orchids   WILLARD CLAY

" The first sign of spring in Virginia is the changing of the light, as dramatic as the changing of the guard at Buckingham Palace, only subtler. Even without going out, even before getting up in the morning, almost without having to open your eyes, you can tell spring is in Virginia. The branches out the window are as bare, but the light that plays over them has a promise, as if the light itself would blossom shortly. "

Guy Friddell,
What Is It about Virginia?

Male Baltimore oriole above its deep, pendant nest   JOHN M. COFFMAN

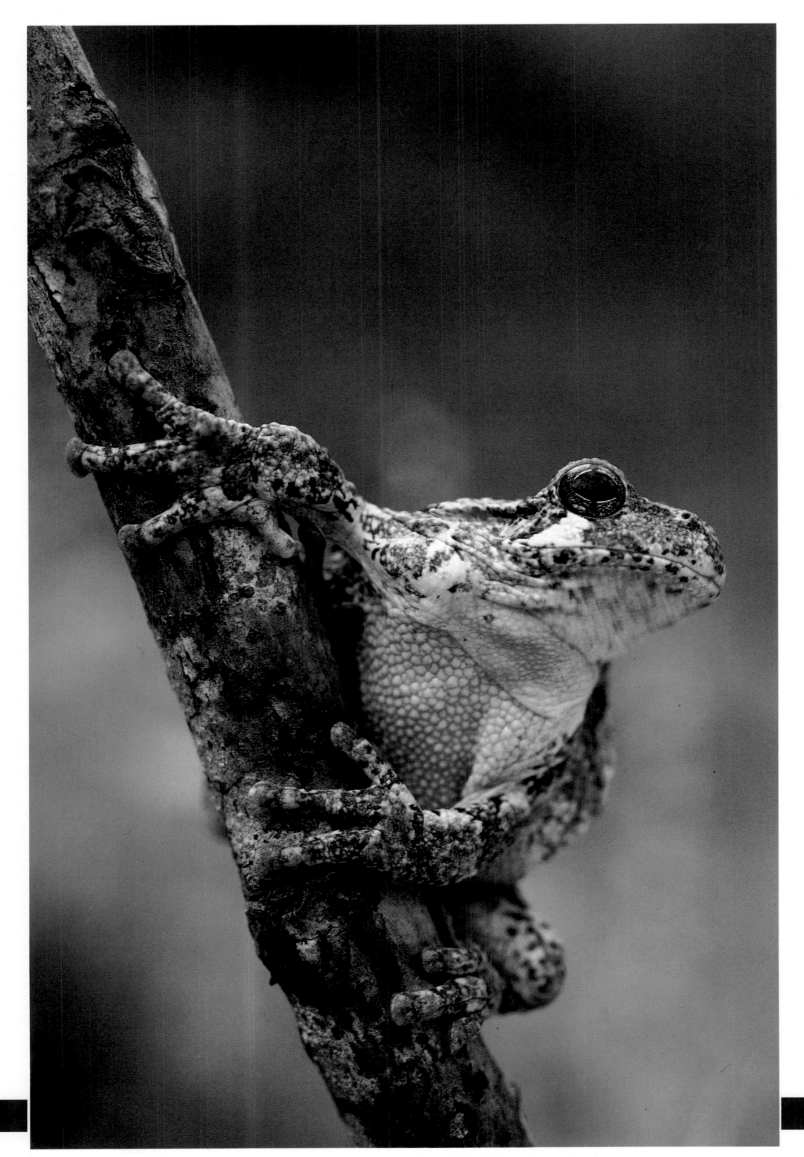

Gray tree frog, a seldom seen but frequently heard resident of Virginia's moist woodlands STEVEN Q. CROY

Matched pair of Canada geese investigating a coastal pond   LYNDA RICHARDSON

“ If today one should wonder how that Tidewater countryside appeared to Washington's eyes, the answer is: much as it does now. For to a degree largely unmatched in America, the region resembles in topography its ancient, earliest configuration. ”

William Styron,
The Quiet Dust

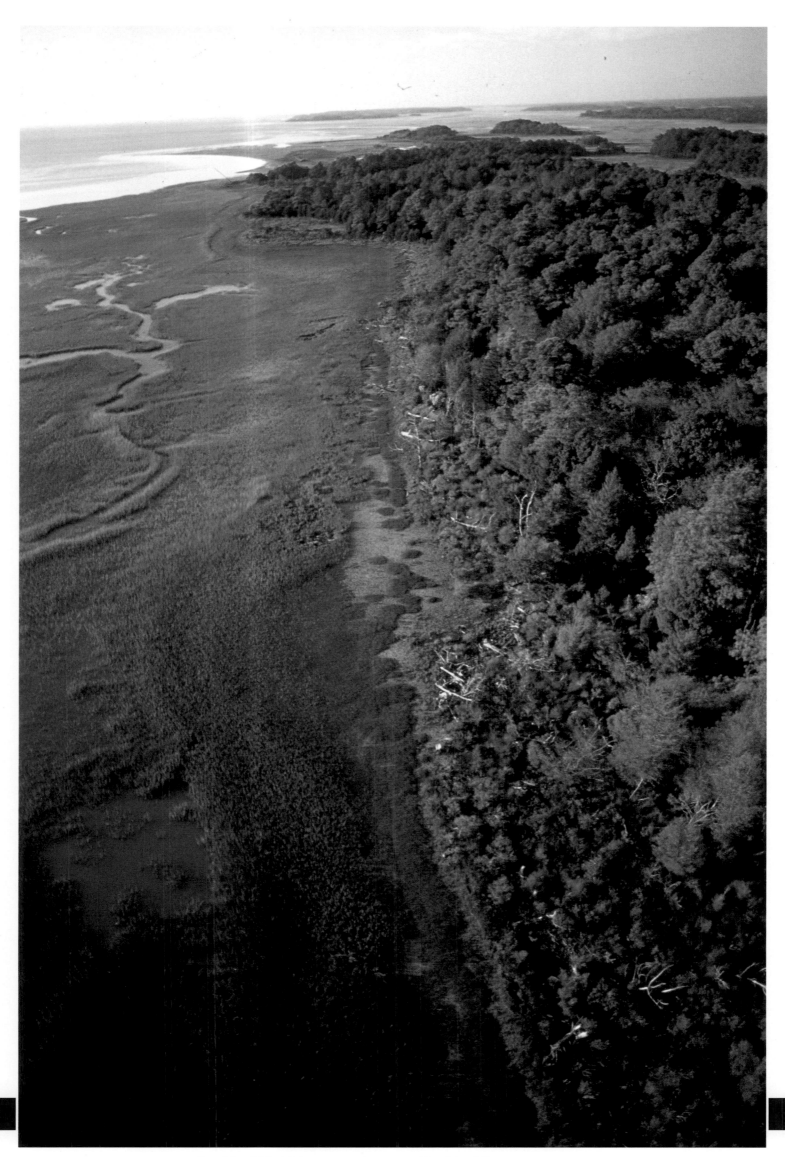

Seaside of Virginia's eastern shore near Hog Island Bay   JOHN M. HALL

An idyllic day at Virginia Beach seems to lure sculptured fish inland   STEVE EARLEY/THE VIRGINIAN-PILOT

"The ocean… comes in bands, violet at the horizon, almost blending with the light-filled sky; turning to deep blue a little lower as it secures its own domain; then green nearing shore, and, finally, taking on a golden tint as it shakes out in rolling white combers on the brown sand of the beach."

Guy Friddell,
What Is It about Virginia?

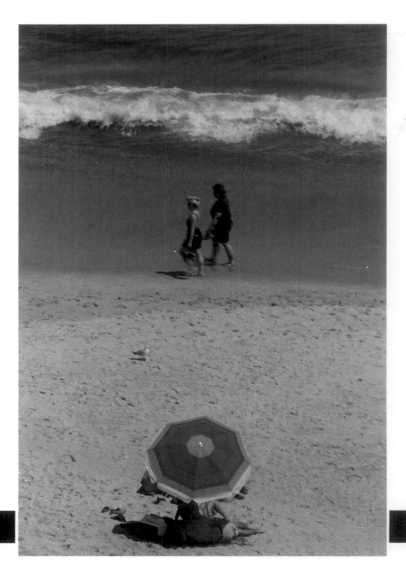

Enjoying the oceanfront, shade or shine
DAVID B. HOLLINGSWORTH/THE VIRGINIAN-PILOT

Roiling combers stroke the shore at Sandbridge in Virginia Beach   CECELIA JOLLEY/THE VIRGINIAN-PILOT

Lord of the longboard   MARTIN SMITH-RODDEN/THE VIRGINIAN-PILOT

Common egrets at rest and play in Chincoteague National Wildlife Refuge, Assateague Island   GLENN VAN NIMWEGEN

" *. . . Assateague belonged to the wild things—to the wild birds that nested on it, and the wild ponies whose ancestors had lived on it since the days of the Spanish galleon.* **"**

Marguerite Henry,
Misty of Chincoteague

21

Wetlands along the northern end of Assateague Island ROBERT PERRON

Pony roll on Assateague Island   D. L. WINSTON

A wild filly steps out on Assateague   D. L. WINSTON

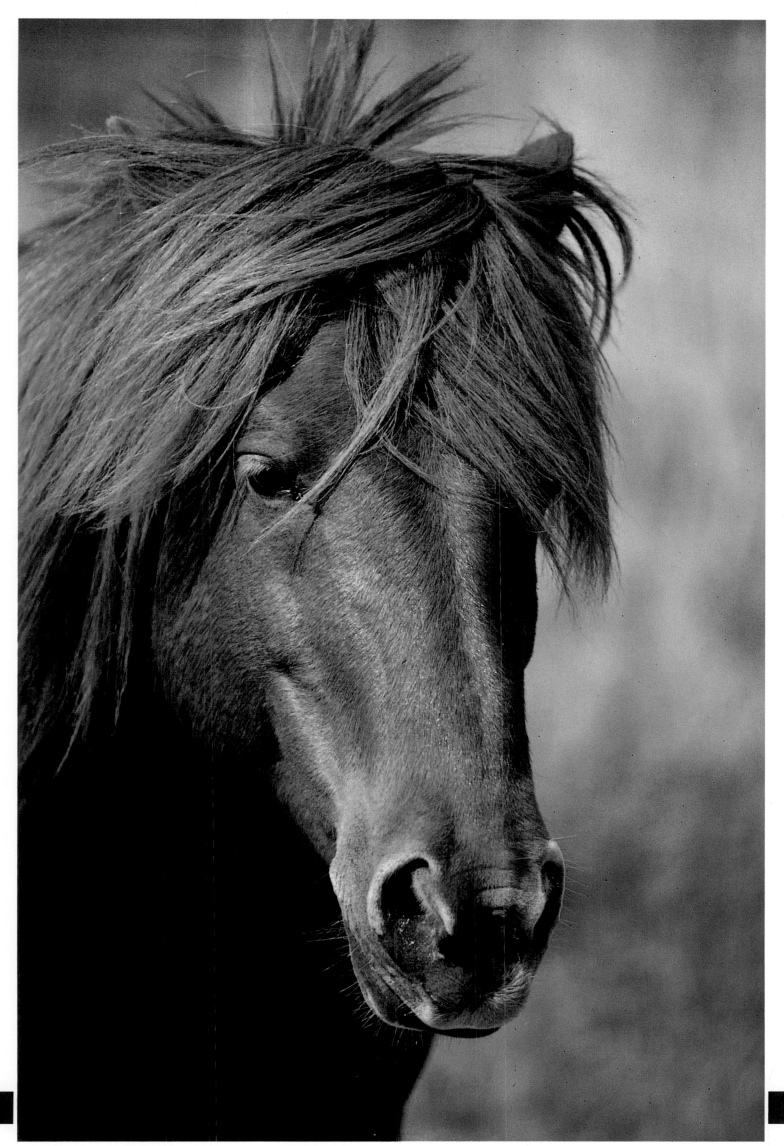

Handsome descendant of Spanish mustangs, Assateague Island   ZIG LESZCZYNSKI / ANIMALS ANIMALS

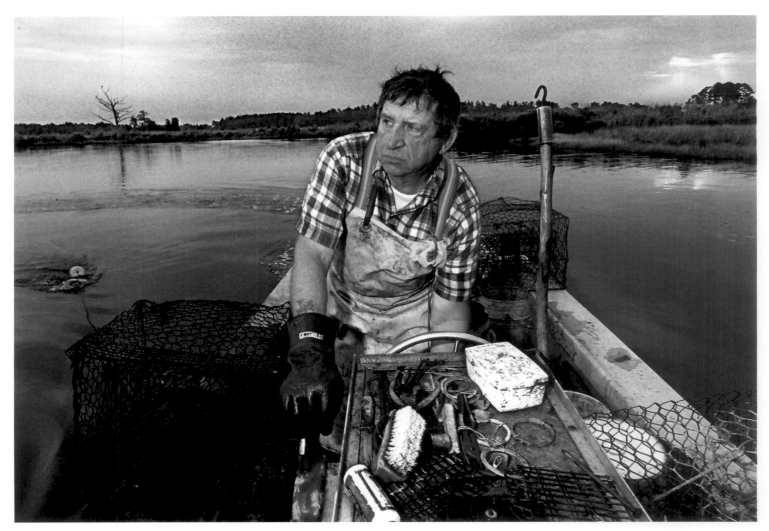

Crabbing on New Mill Creek at Chesapeake   MORT FRYMAN/THE VIRGINIAN-PILOT

" *The Shore is like a table… lying off the coast of Virginia, heaped with all kinds of fresh vegetables, and lapped with fish spilling every which way, like a groaning board in a Flemish painting.* **"**

Guy Friddell,
We Began at Jamestown

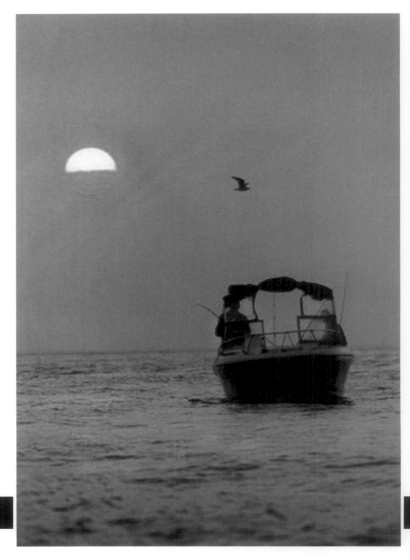

Hoping to snag their limit of strip bass on Chesapeake Bay
DAVID B. HOLLINGSWORTH/THE VIRGINIAN-PILOT

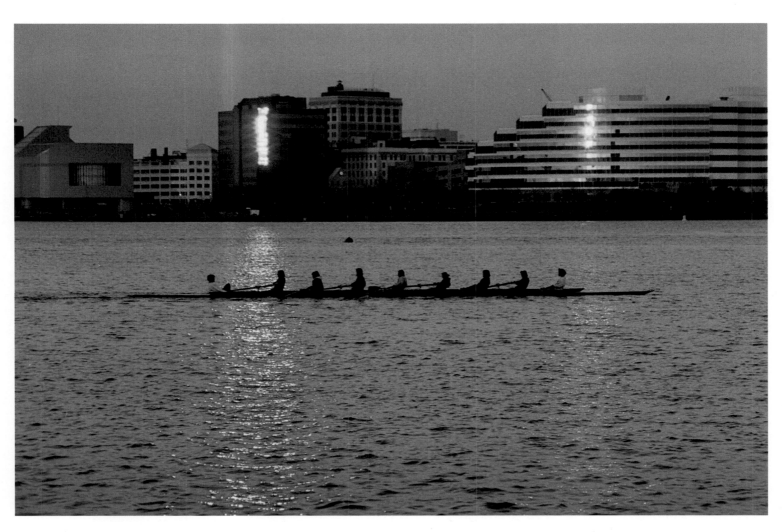

Dedicated Portsmouth rowers put in a long day practicing for an upcoming race   JIM WALKER/THE VIRGINIAN-PILOT

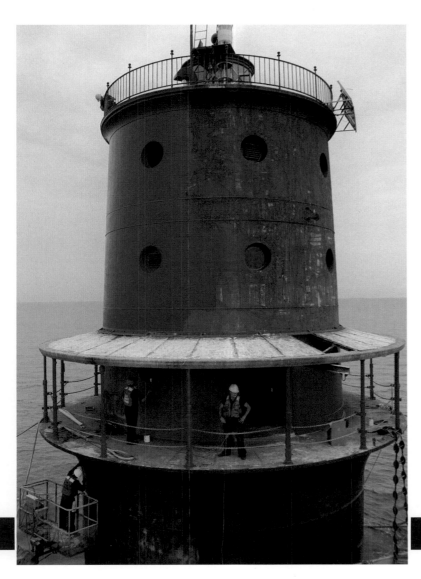

A Coast Guard crew spruces up the Thimble Shoal Lighthouse at Norfolk
D. KEVIN ELLIOTT/THE VIRGINIAN-PILOT

A winter day makes a memorable exit at Back Bay National Wildlife Refuge   CECELIA JOLLEY/THE VIRGINIAN-PILOT

*" This is a noble sea. Calm and hospitable,
majestic in size. Its potential cannot be imagined. "*

Captain John Smith

Red sky in morning, sailors take warning MAE SCANLAN

Virginia Beach CATHERINE KARNOW

Summer fun on Buckroe Beach in Hampton   CATHERINE KARNOW

You can never have too much suntan lotion   CATHERINE KARNOW

The devil-may-care atmosphere of the beach is enough to make this pair lose their heads   BILL TIERNAN/THE VIRGINIAN-PILOT

" *[T]he chief attraction [of the beach] is the scope it offers anybody to play as a child, or even a fool. You cannot simply run for fun along a downtown street, at least not without pretending to chase a bus, nor can you sit down and construct a castle on the curb, even if there were sand…. But almost any antic is accepted on the beach.* **"**

Guy Friddell,
What Is It about Virginia?

Personal watercraft ply the waters of Chesapeake Bay
GARY C. KNAPP/THE VIRGINIAN-PILOT

Skateboarders properly attired at Virginia Beach   CATHERINE KARNOW

"I'd give up my other tooth for a bite."   CATHERINE KARNOW

Savoring the view at Virginia Beach   CATHERINE KARNOW

Rolling in from the frothy Atlantic   MAE SCANLAN

"Chaos! The surf seems to bellow as it explodes rhythmically against the beach here. And the beach whispers back, ever so improbably—order."

Tom Horton,
Bay Country

Faces only a mother could love   D. KEVIN ELLIOTT/THE VIRGINIAN-PILOT

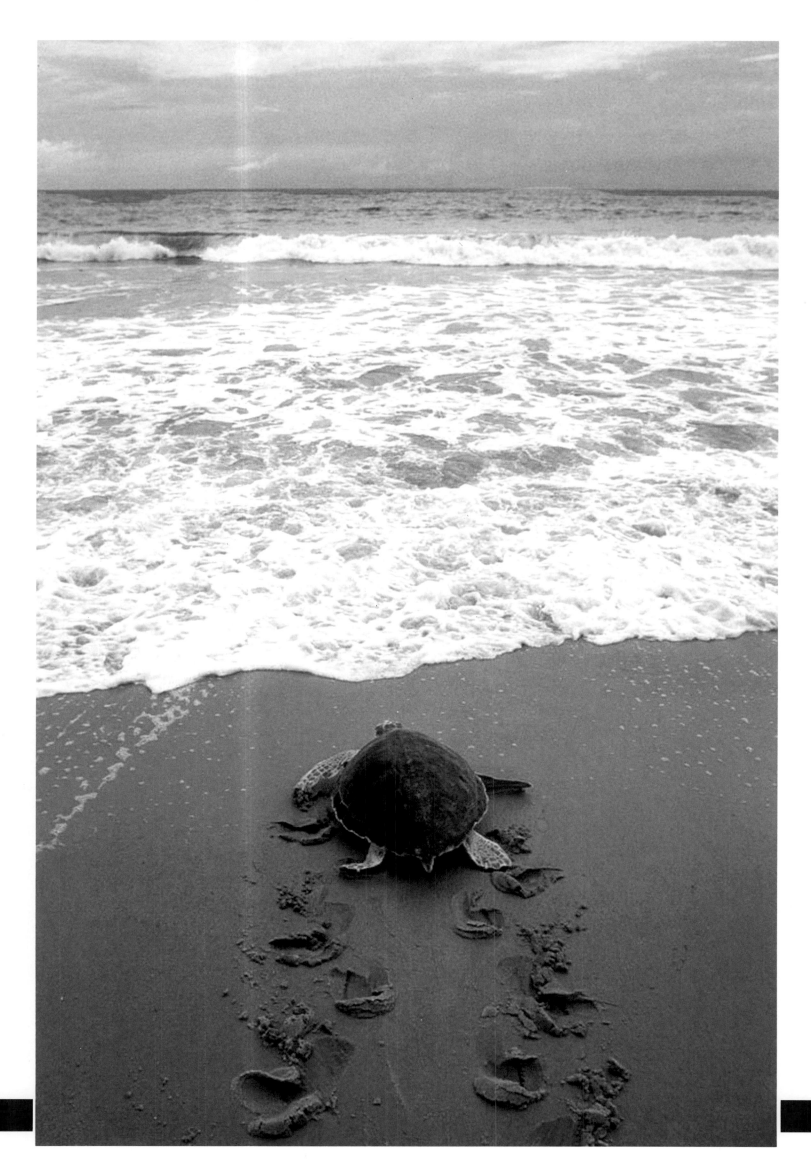

Heeding the enigmatic call of the sea   CHRISTOPHER REDDICK/THE VIRGINIAN-PILOT

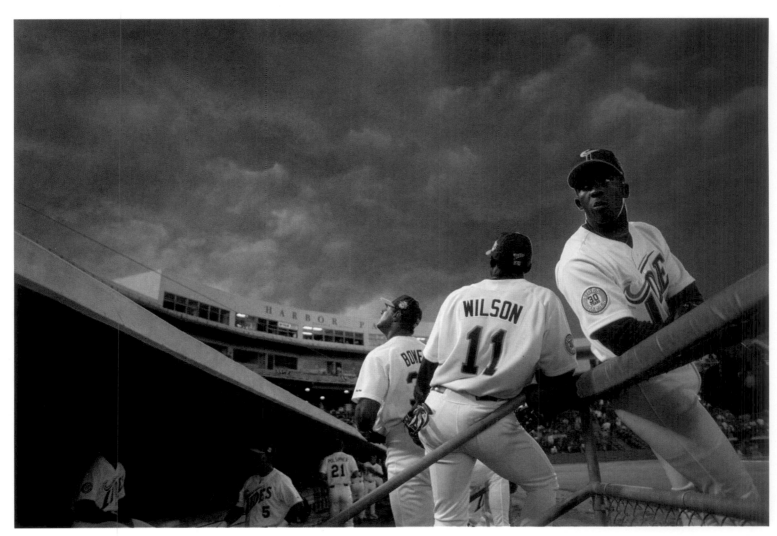

Nature threatens to cancel a Norfolk Tides-Durham Bulls game   NHAT MEYER/THE VIRGINIAN-PILOT

Burning rubber at Virginia Motorsports Park in Dinwiddie   VICKI CRONIS/THE VIRGINIAN-PILOT

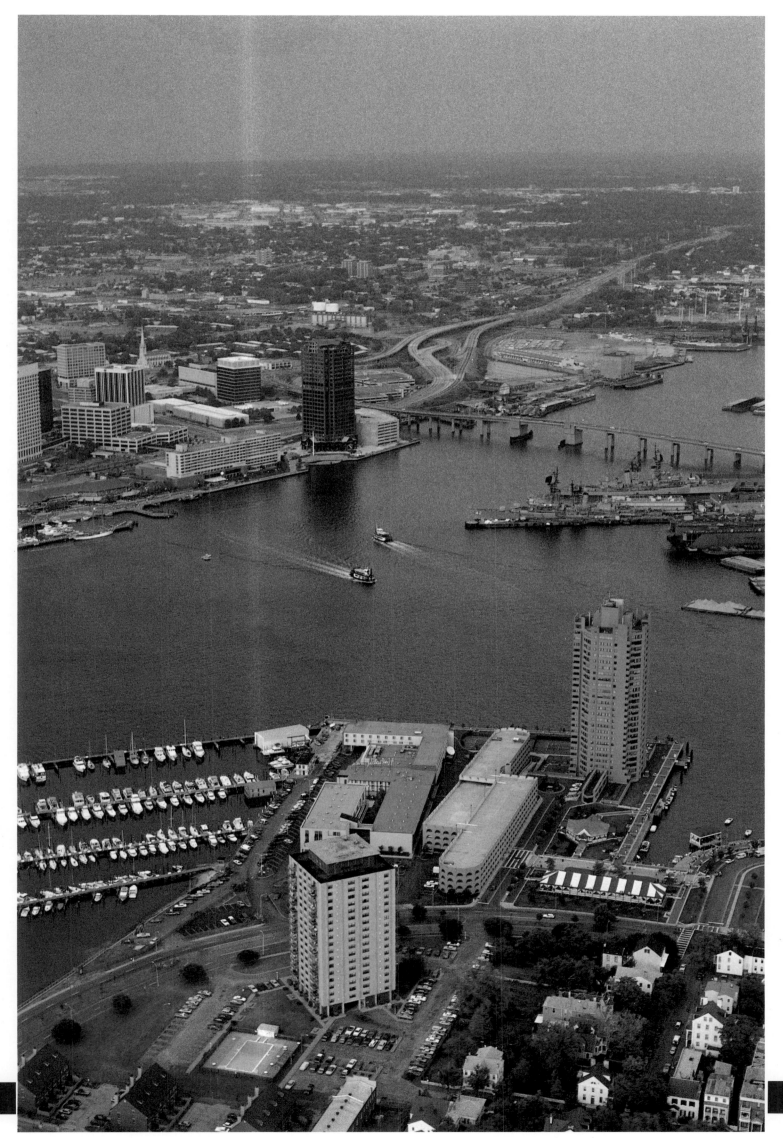

Portsmouth (foreground) and Norfolk, near the mouth of Hampton Roads   CATHERINE KARNOW

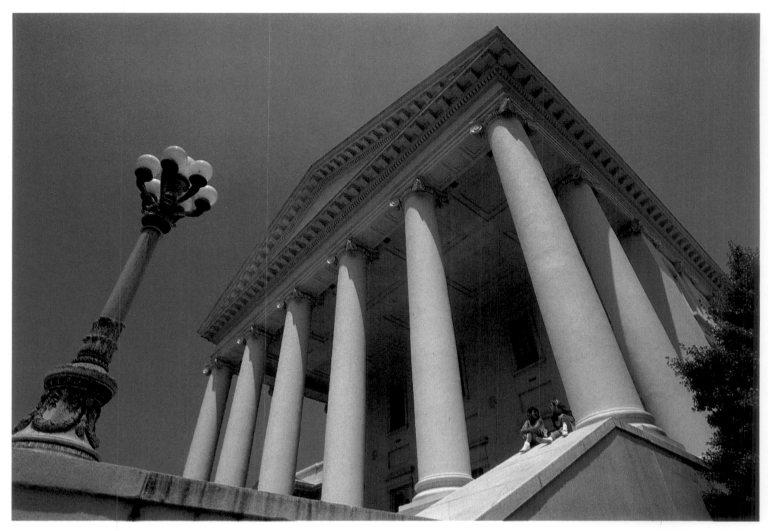

The State Capitol, serving Virginia since 1788   CATHERINE KARNOW

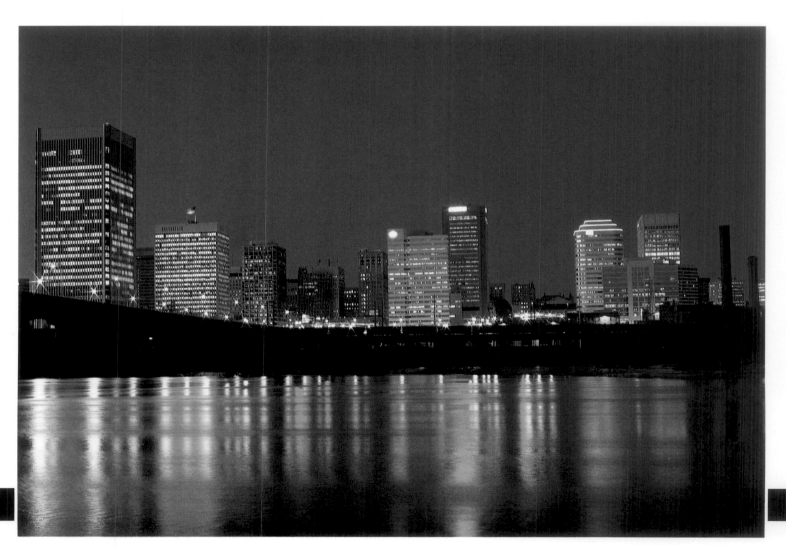

Richmond skyline from across the James River   CATHERINE KARNOW

Scottish dancers from Nova Scotia entertain at a Norfolk festival   LAWRENCE JACKSON/THE VIRGINIAN-PILOT

A lesson in art appreciation at the Chrysler Museum in Norfolk
JIM WALKER/THE VIRGINIAN-PILOT

Family outing at Maymont Park in Richmond   CATHERINE KARNOW

Worshippers decked in their finest at the Hindu Temple, Hampton Roads   STEVE EARLEY/THE VIRGINIAN-PILOT

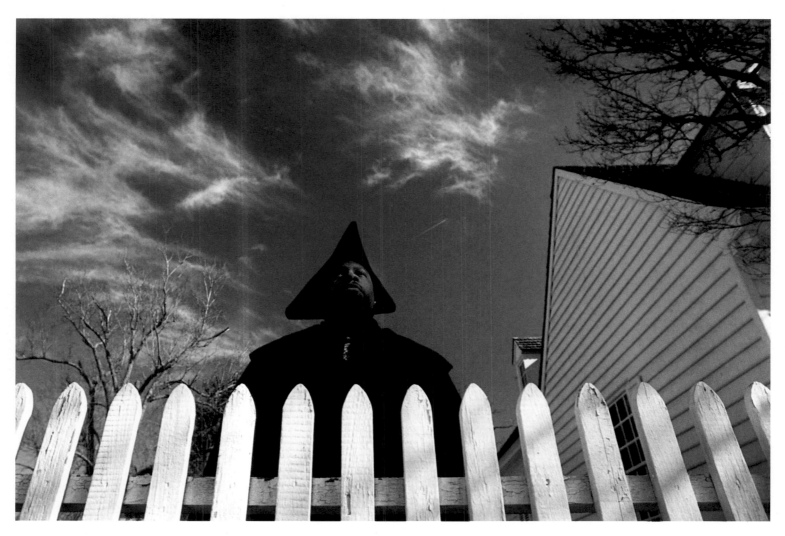

A re-enactor in historical dress at the Brush-Everard House in Colonial Williamsburg   MARTIN SMITH-RODDEN/THE VIRGINIAN-PILOT

A powwow participant undergoing a rite of purification   MICHAEL KESTNER/THE VIRGINIAN-PILOT

Oak-guarded Westover Plantation, built in 1734 and still resplendent, east of Richmond   DEREK FELL

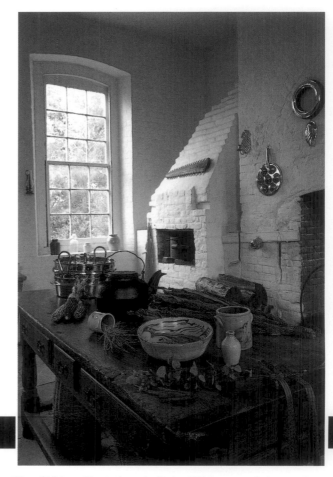

The Shirley Plantation, built in 1724, one of the earliest
tobacco plantations in the New World   CATHERINE KARNOW

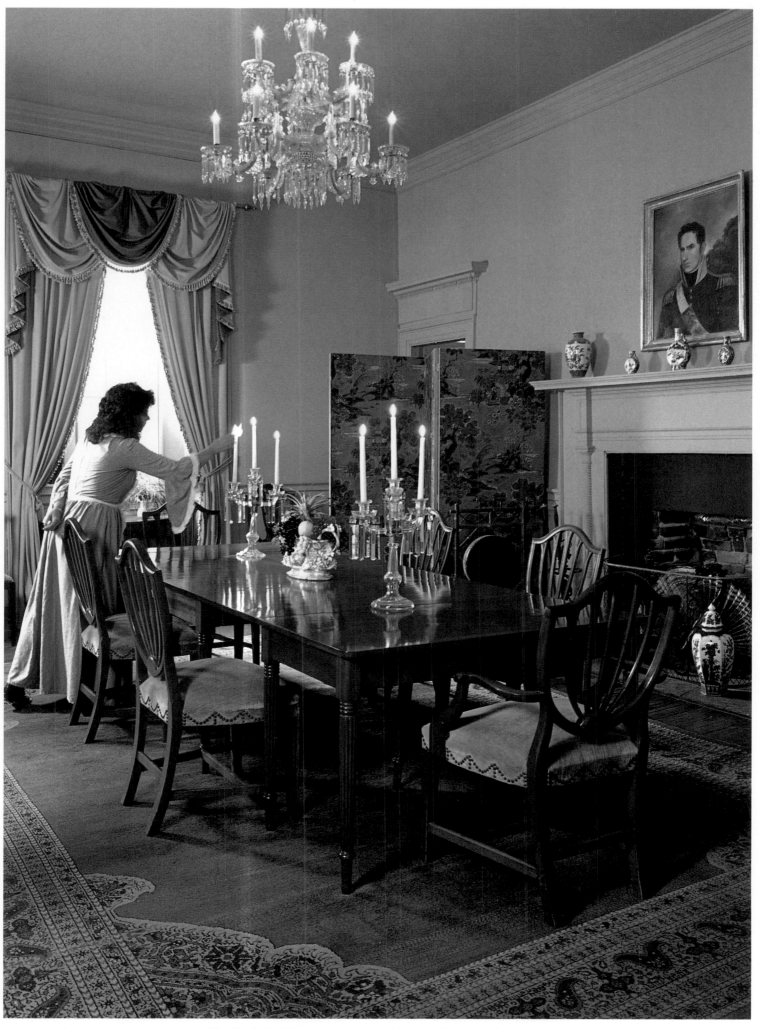

The Berkeley Plantation, ancestral home of two presidents—
William Henry Harrison and his grandson, Benjamin Harrison   CATHERINE KARNOW

Green tree frog in full voice on a pickerelweed leaf   FREDRICK D. ATWOOD

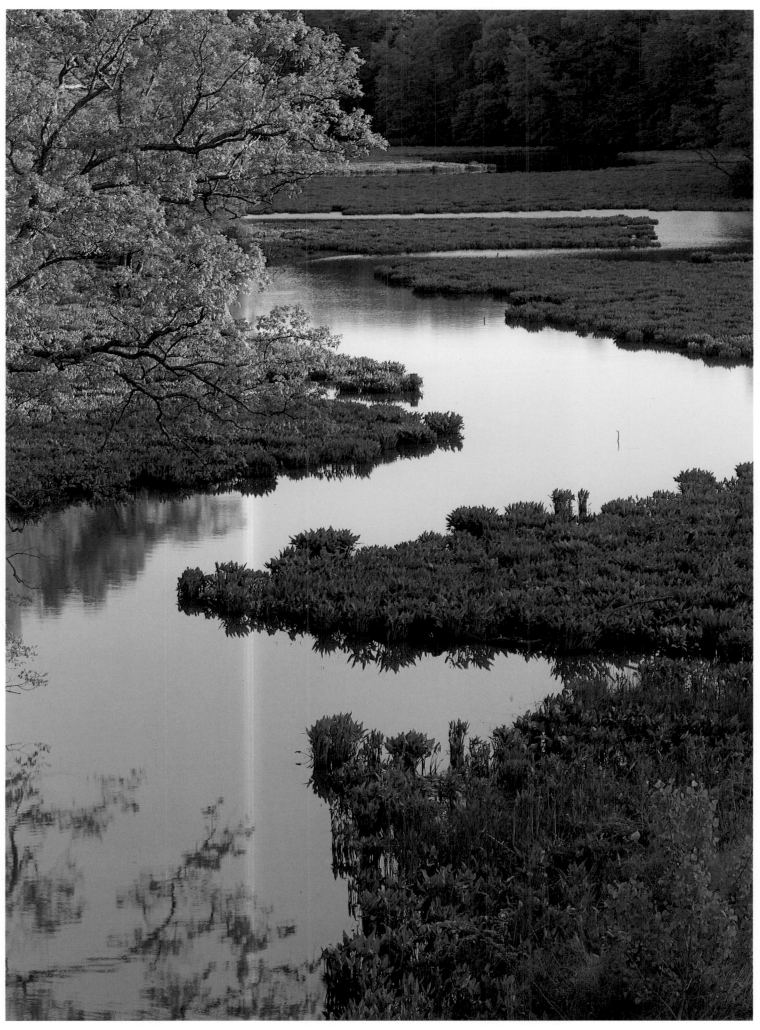

Freshwater marsh from the Colonial Parkway, along the James River   DAVID MUENCH

Sailors at Norfolk Naval Base celebrate many happy returns   MOTOYA NAKAMURA/THE VIRGINIAN-PILOT

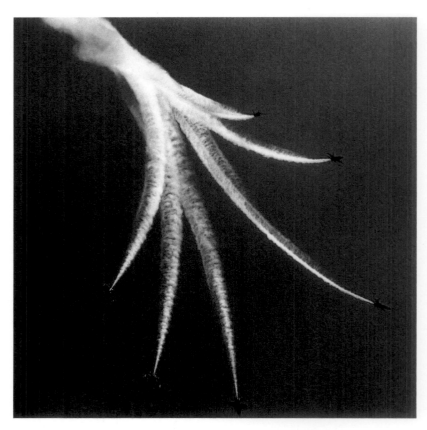

The Blue Angels delight spectactors at a Norfolk Naval Base air show
MOTOYA NAKAMURA/THE VIRGINIAN-PILOT

Poignant reunions are the order of the day at Norfolk   MOTOYA NAKAMURA/THE VIRGINIAN-PILOT

" *There is such a thing as honor. Virginians have lived for it, died for it....* **"**

Virginia Moore,
Virginia Is a State of Mind

Shenandoah Valley farm   JEFF GNASS

> **To define the Shenandoah is an impossible and an unnecessary task. It is better merely to admire it, and to select here and there a dimple or a contour that catches our fancy.**
>
> **Wallace Nutting,**
> Virginia Beautiful

Colorful mementos of summer's bounty   STEVE EARLEY/THE VIRGINIAN-PILOT

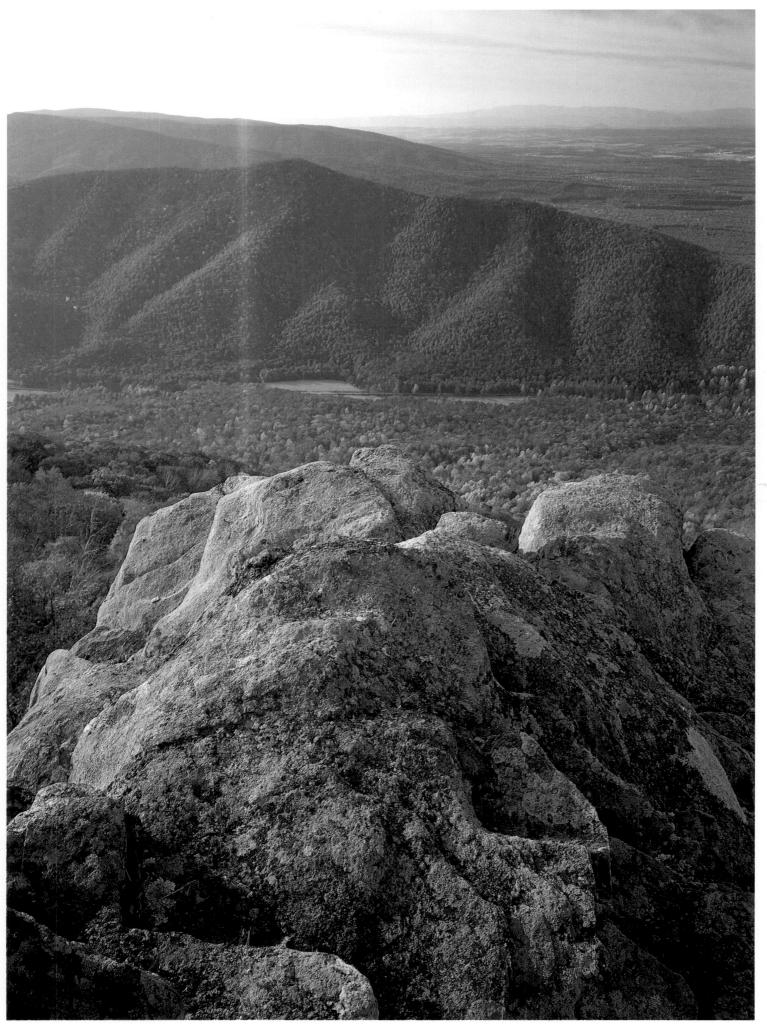

Colors of fall across the Shenandoah Valley   CARR CLIFTON

Virginia's state flower and tree, the dogwood   WILLARD CLAY

" *Mountains are giant, restful, absorbent. You can heave your spirit into a mountain and the mountain will keep it, folded, and not throw it back as some creeks will. The creeks are the world with all its stimulus and beauty; I live there. But the mountains are home.* "

Annie Dillard,
Pilgrim at Tinker Creek

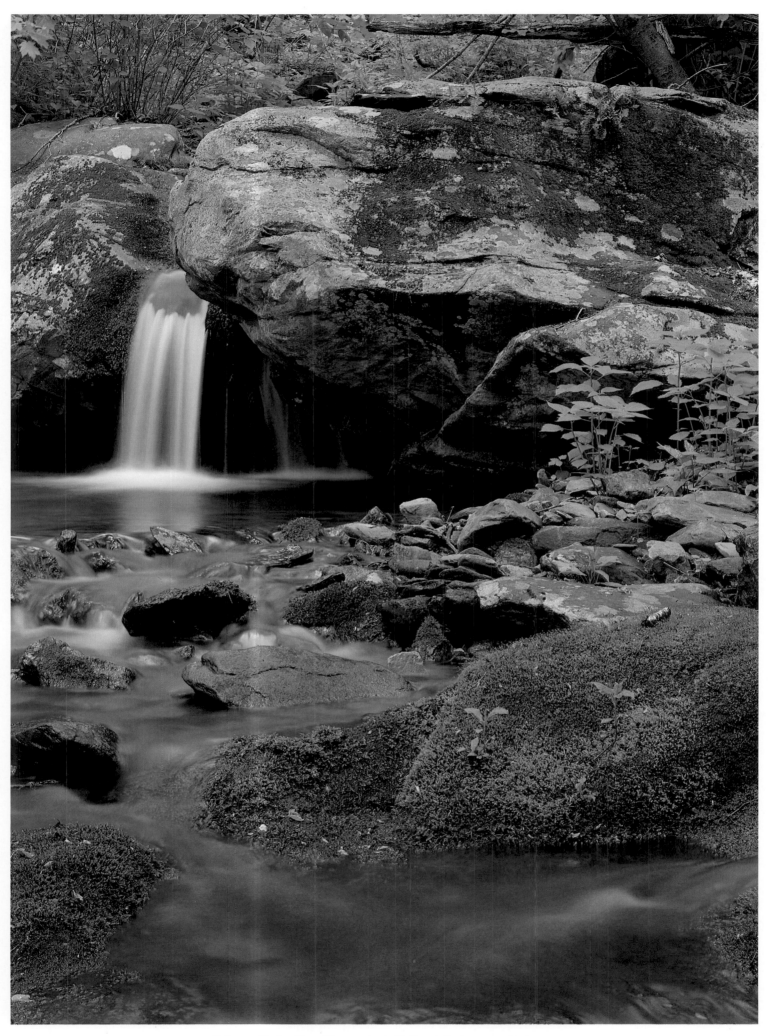

Falls on Cedar Run, Shenandoah National Park   WILLARD CLAY

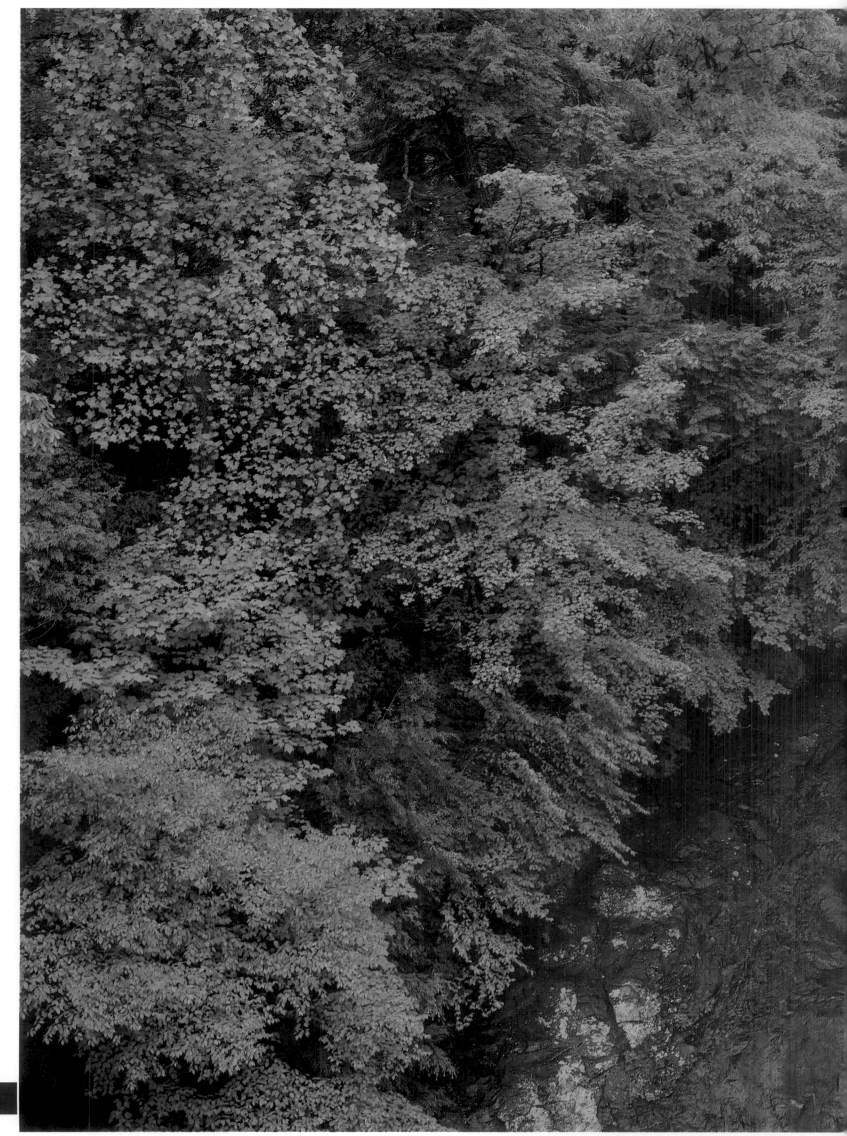

White Oak Run cascading through White Oak Canyon, Shenandoah National Park   WILLARD CLAY

Unknown soldier's grave,
Arlington National Cemetery   MAE SCANLAN

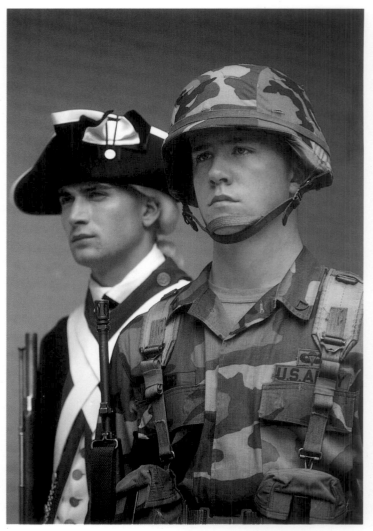

Members of the Old Guard, past and present
WILLIAM B. FOLSOM / ARMY MAGAZINE

" *No other cemetery can compare to Arlington. The list of
persons buried there is an index to the Nation's history* **"**

Guy Friddell,
The Virginia Way

Iwo Jima Memorial in Arlington   CATHERINE KARNOW

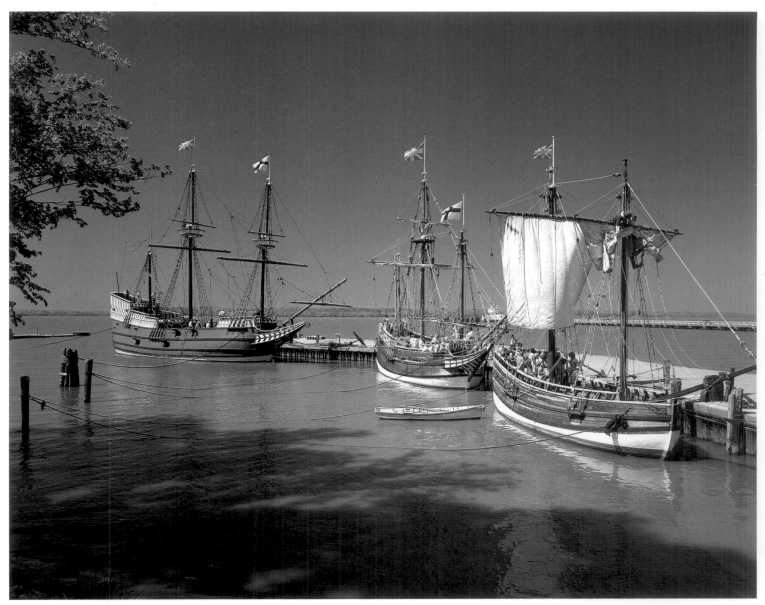

The *Susan Constant, Discovery,* and *Godspeed,* replicas of settlers' ships, docked at Jamestown Festival Park   TOM ALGIRE

66 *. . . the Countrie (for the moste part) on each side plaine high ground, with many fresh Springes, the people in all places kindely intreating us, daunsing and feasting us with strawberries Mulberies, Bread, Fish, and other their Countrie provisions wherof we had plenty. . .* 99

Captain John Smith,
1607

Passmore Creek on Jamestown Island   MAE SCANLAN

Church tower at Jamestown, erected in 1639 and the oldest brick structure in the United States   MAE SCANLAN

A settler's view of sunset over the James River, Jamestown National Historic Site   MAE SCANLAN

Grocer's sign, Williamsburg STEVE SOLUM

Aiming to bring history alive at Colonial Williamsburg BILL TIERNAN/THE VIRGINIAN-PILOT

The 18th-century Governor's Palace in Williamsburg, grandly illuminated   MARTIN SMITH-RODDEN/THE VIRGINIAN-PILOT

Preparing a colonial meal at the Governor's Palace   JOHN LEWIS STAGE / THE IMAGE BANK

Muskets and bayonets, functional wall decorations at the Governor's Palace   JAMES FRANK

The Magazine, built in 1715 to house guns, ammunition, and gunpowder at Williamsburg   DAVID MUENCH

" *The more I have ranged the country the more I admire it. I have seen the best countries in Europe; I protest unto you, before the living God, put them all together, (and) this country will be equivalent unto them if it be inhabit(ed) with good people.* "

Sir Thomas Dale,
1613

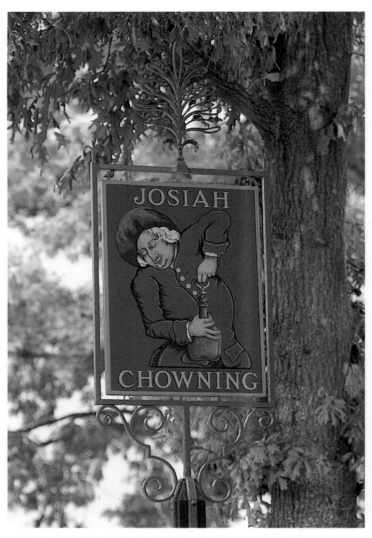

Cheers at Chowning's, Williamsburg   CATHERINE KARNOW

Cobblers at work   JOHN LEWIS STAGE / THE IMAGE BANK

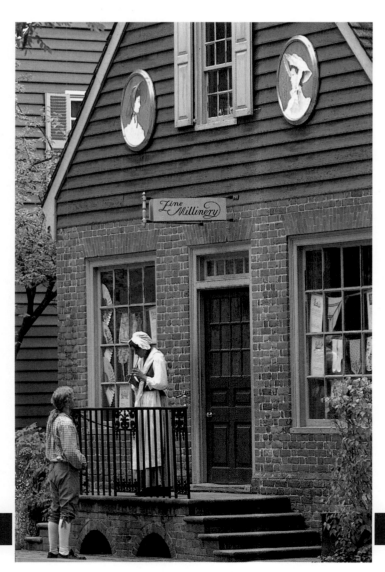

Fine millinery and fine flute music, Williamsburg
CATHERINE KARNOW

❝ *The most eloquent testimony to Virginia's future lay all about us... in the golden triangle of history formed by Jamestown, Yorktown, and Williamsburg.* **❞**

Guy Friddell,
What Is It about Virginia?

A wide-angle view of Alexandria City Hall, built in 1817 and rebuilt after a fire in 1871   CATHERINE KARNOW

Toy shop in Alexandria   CATHERINE KARNOW

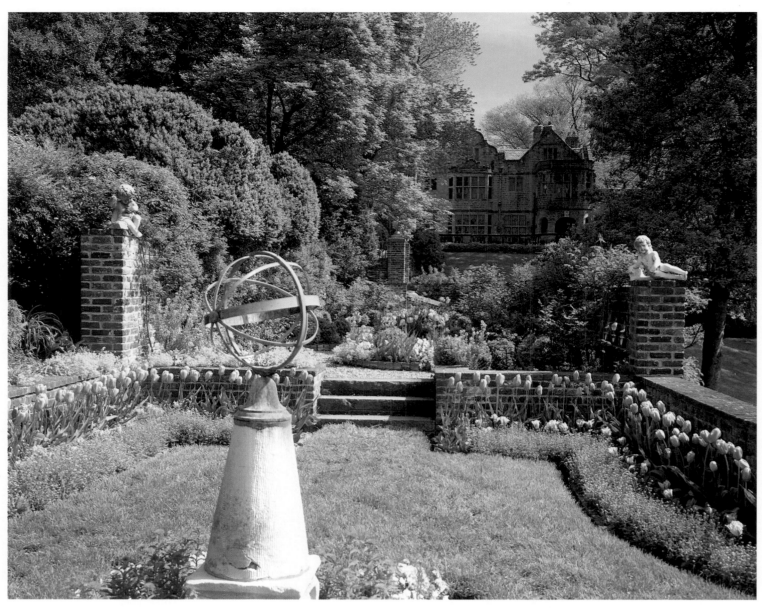

Gardens at Virginia House, a 12th-century monastery shipped from England
and reassembled in Virginia in the 1920s by U.S. Ambassador Alexander Weddell   GENE AHRENS

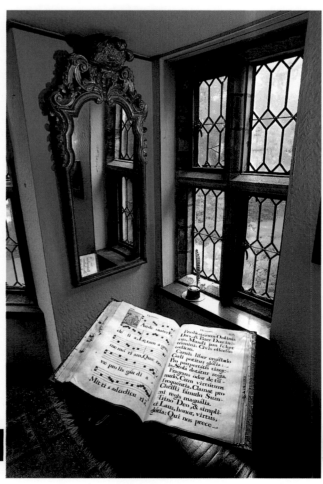

Interior of Virginia House   CATHERINE KARNOW

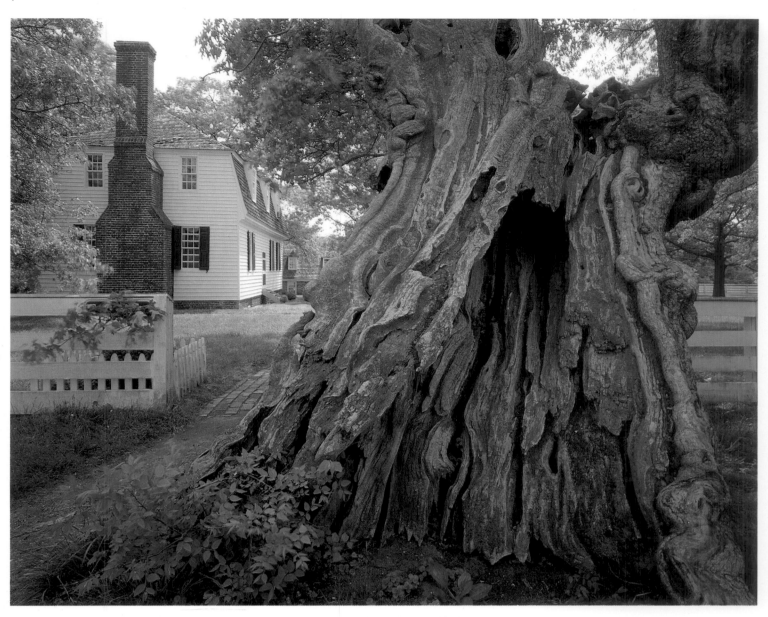

The old mulberry tree at the Moore House, Yorktown   DAVID MUENCH

The surrender room in the Moore House, where Lord Cornwallis surrendered to General Washington in 1781   CONNIE TOOPS

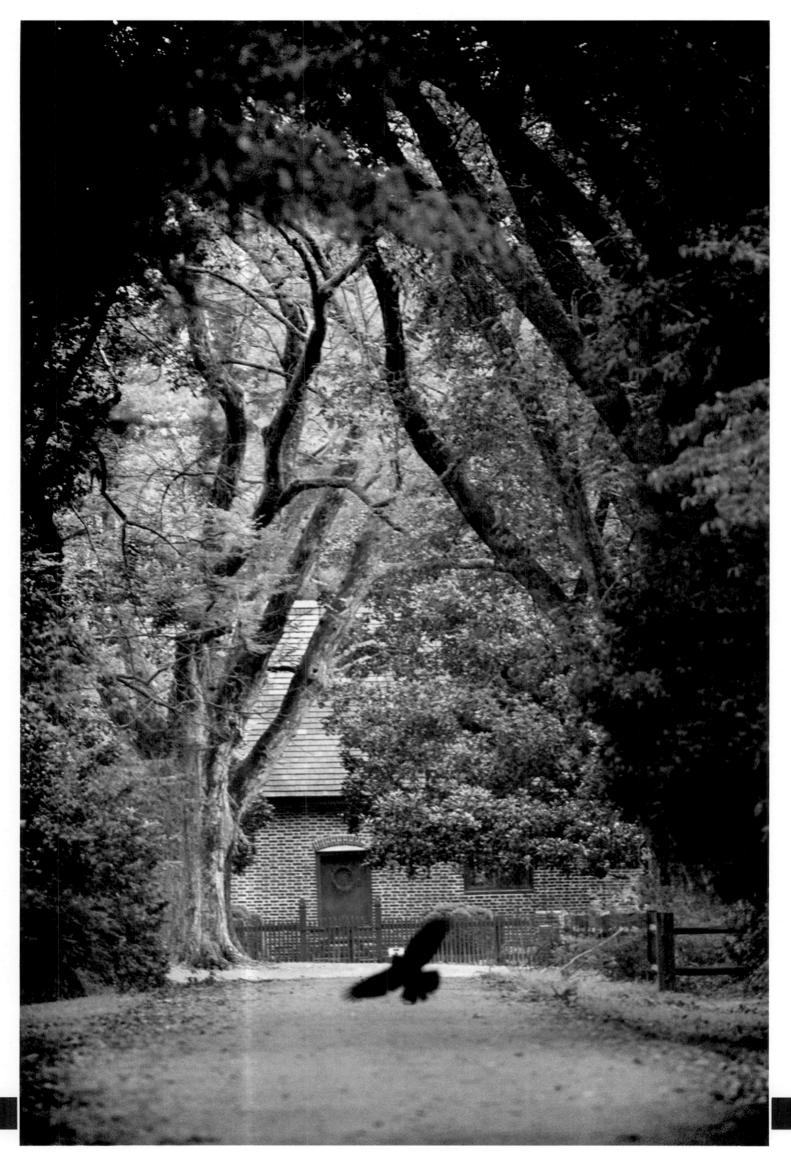

The Adam Thoroughgood House, built circa 1680 in Virginia Beach   DAVID B. HOLLINGSWOFTH/THE VIRGINIAN-PILOT

Monticello, Thomas Jefferson's beloved home   DAVID MUENCH

" *I am as happy nowhere else and in no other society, and all my wishes end, where I hope my days will end, at Monticello.* "

Thomas Jefferson,
1789

Bust of Jefferson at the University of Virginia   MAE SCANLAN

A portion of the grounds at Mount Vernon   MAE SCANLAN

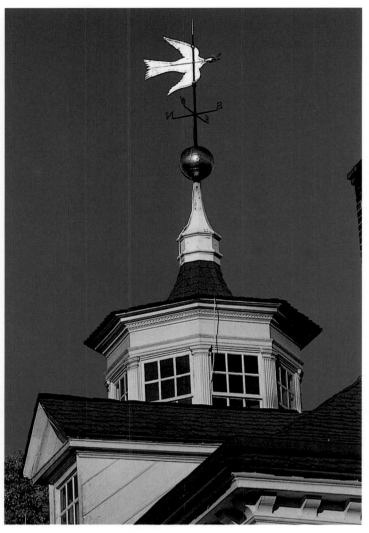

Cupola atop Mount Vernon   CATHERINE KARNOW

Mount Vernon   MAE SCANLAN

" I can truly say I had rather be at Mount Vernon with a friend or two about me, than to be attended at the seat of government by the officers of state and the representatives of every power in Europe. "

George Washington,
letter written in 1790

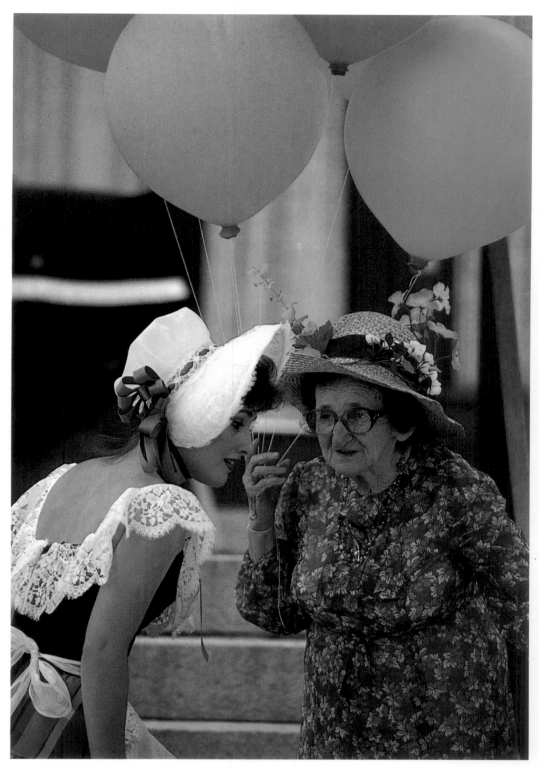

Easter bonnets and belles in Richmond   TIM WRIGHT

« Virginians are the most unmitigated, incorrigible, thoroughgoing, unqualified, consummate, whole-hog, glaring, flagrant, enormous, fabulous, perfect, stark, radical, downright, pure, headlong, rampant, irregardless, tooth-and-nail, devil-may-care, bull-at-the-gate individualists in the world. If you do not know this, you will never know Virginians. It is the key to their character. And this, I claim, is a phenomenon at a time when 'the individual withers and the world is more and more.' »

Virginia Moore,
Virginia Is a State of Mind

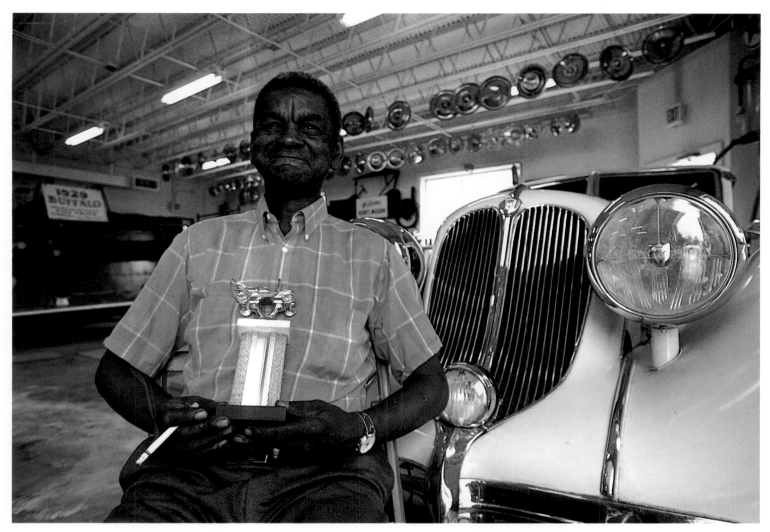

Shiny trophies and antique automobiles at Rohr's Antiques in Manassas CATHERINE KARNOW

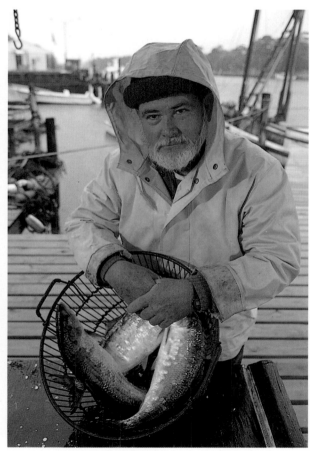

A day's catch, Norfolk CATHERINE KARNOW

Aboard the *Caper* at Norfolk CATHERINE KARNOW

A local bicycle race in McLean   WILLIAM B. FOLSOM

Off and running at the Richmond Marathon   P.A. GORMAS

Thrills but no spills at Chesapeake Park   GARY C. KNAPP/THE VIRGINIAN-PILOT

Great blue heron matching the color of the morning, Assateague Island   GLENN VAN NIMWEGEN

" *...Virginia is the land of the golden mean. The winter begins late and the spring comes early, and there is a gentleness, an unsentimental sweetness in the air...* "

Virginia Moore,
Virginia Is a State of Mind

Birdfoot violet brightening a Virginia wood CONNIE TOOPS

Redbuds decorating the banks of the Shenandoah River   SCOTT T. SMITH

" April and May are the liveliest time of year, when the trees and shrubs of Virginia are in bloom—the soft white and pink dogwood, redbud, wild azalea, crab apple and forsythia. "

Michael Frome,
Virginia

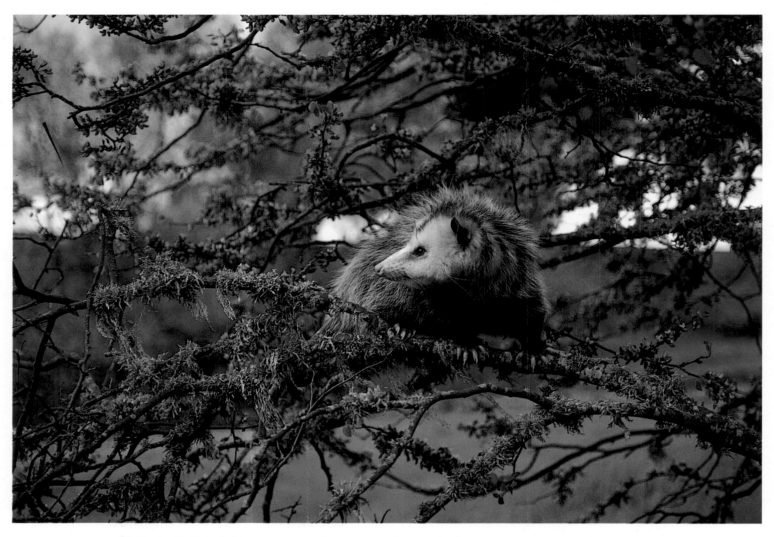

Generally nocturnal, this opossum makes an uncustomary daytime appearance   ERWIN & PEGGY BAUER

Dogwood blossoms—exquisite signs of spring   CHARLIE MEADS/THE VIRGINIAN-PILOT

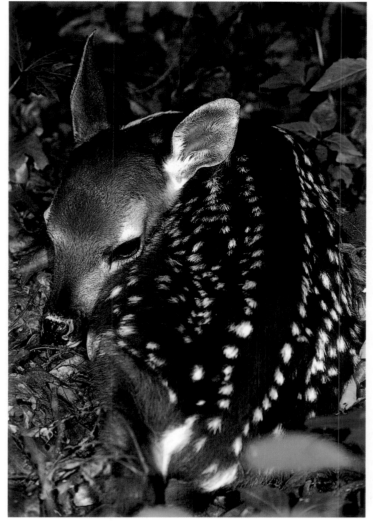

Whitetail fawn   JOHN M. COFFMAN

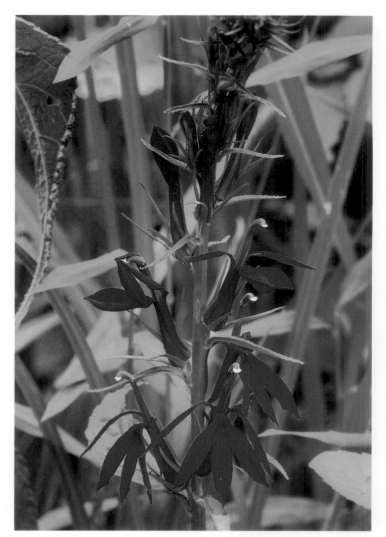

Cardinal flower   JOHN M. COFFMAN

" Spring was running in a thin green flame over the Valley. There was a mist of green on the trees; luminous patches of green and blue sprinkled the earth. The deeper hollows were thatched with shade, and all the little hills, just touched by sunlight, were carved into stillness. "

Ellen Glasgow,
Vein of Iron

Foggy morning in the Blue Ridge Mountains   WILLARD CLAY

Newly hatched box turtle discovering the world   FREDRICK D. ATWOOD

Praying mantis, waiting for the unwary   FREDRICK D. ATWOOD

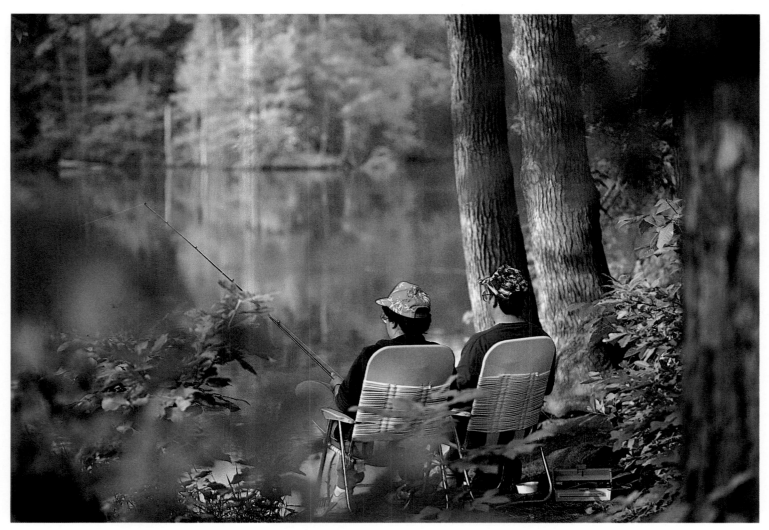

Fishing, Virginia style   CATHERINE KARNOW

Alluring colors   CATHERINE KARNOW

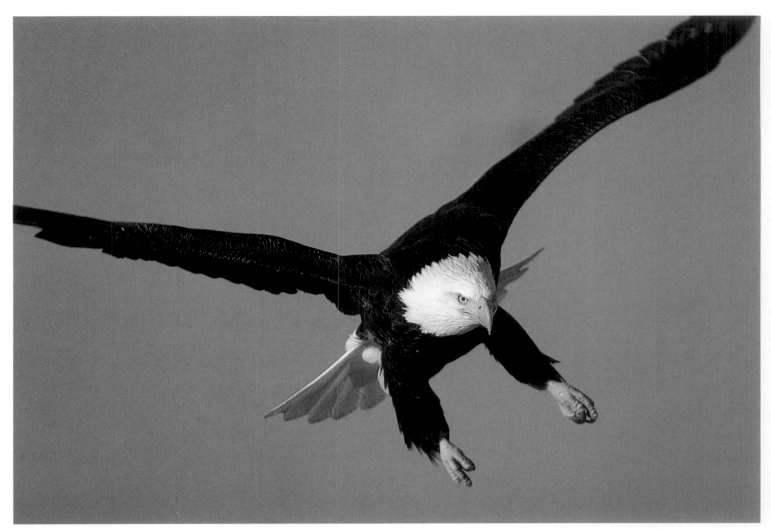

Bald eagle along Virginia's northern coast   FRANK OBERLE / PHOTOGRAPHIC RESOURCES

Bobwhite quail on the lookout   LYNDA RICHARDSON

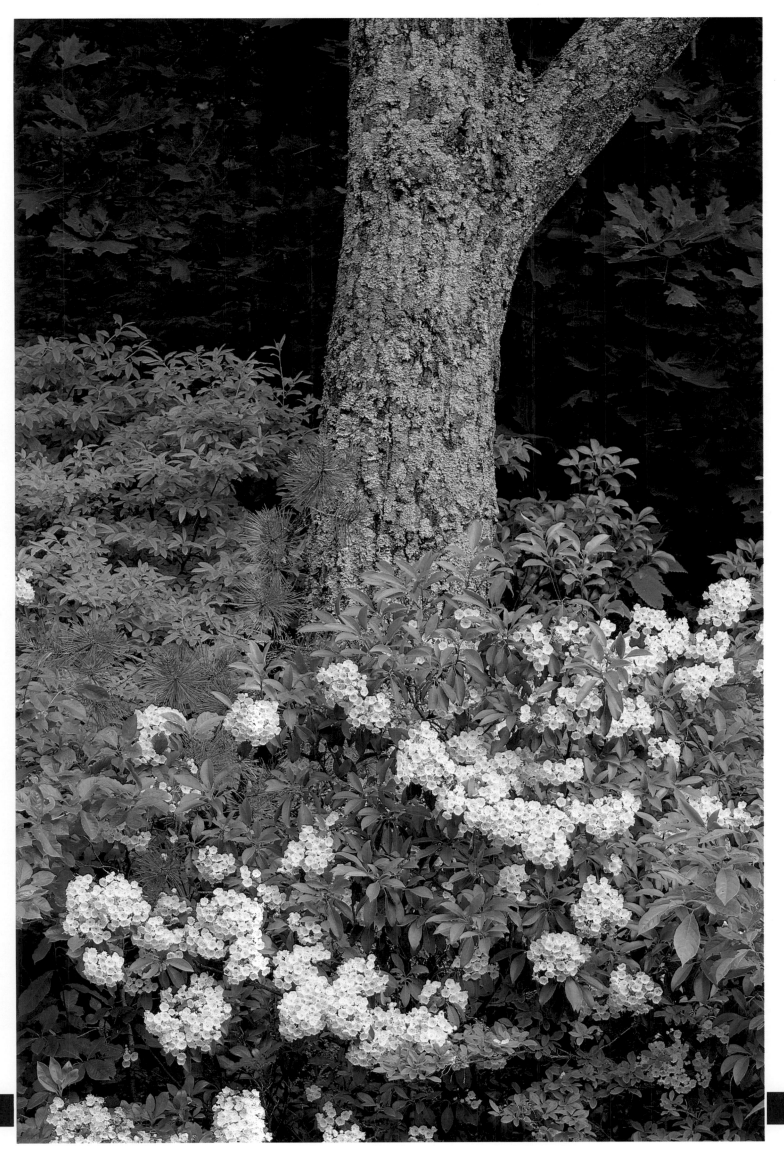

Mountain laurel   WILLARD CLAY

" In the fall the slopes… throng with jostling tribes of trees in blazing war bonnets—yellow hickory, flaming maple, bronze and purple oaks—and the broom sage fields along the Valley floor are dotted with dark green scrub pines, crouching scouts sent out ahead of the multitude of warriors carpeting the mountains, descending in an aura of color. "

Guy Friddell,
What Is It about Virginia?

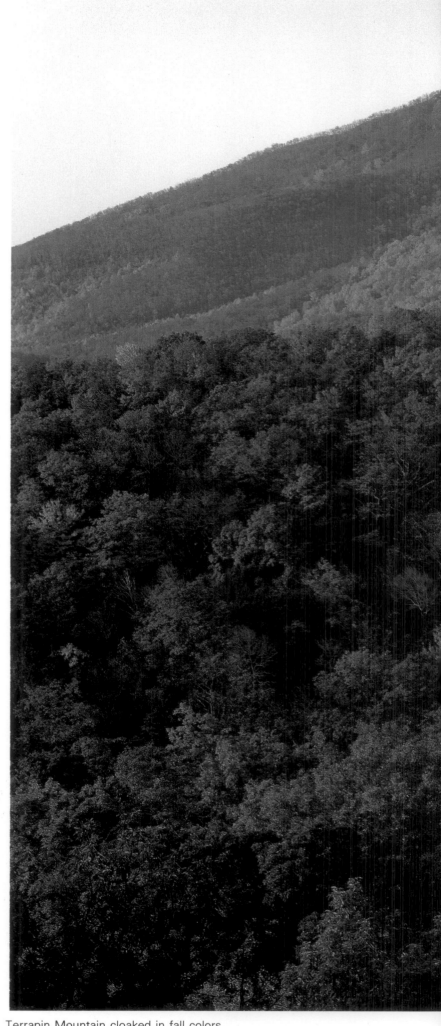

Terrapin Mountain cloaked in fall colors,
Jefferson National Forest near Peaks of Otter   CARR CLIFTON

Autumn mushrooms, Jamestown Island   JEFF GNASS

Chipmunk stuffing itself for the winter   JOHN M. COFFMAN

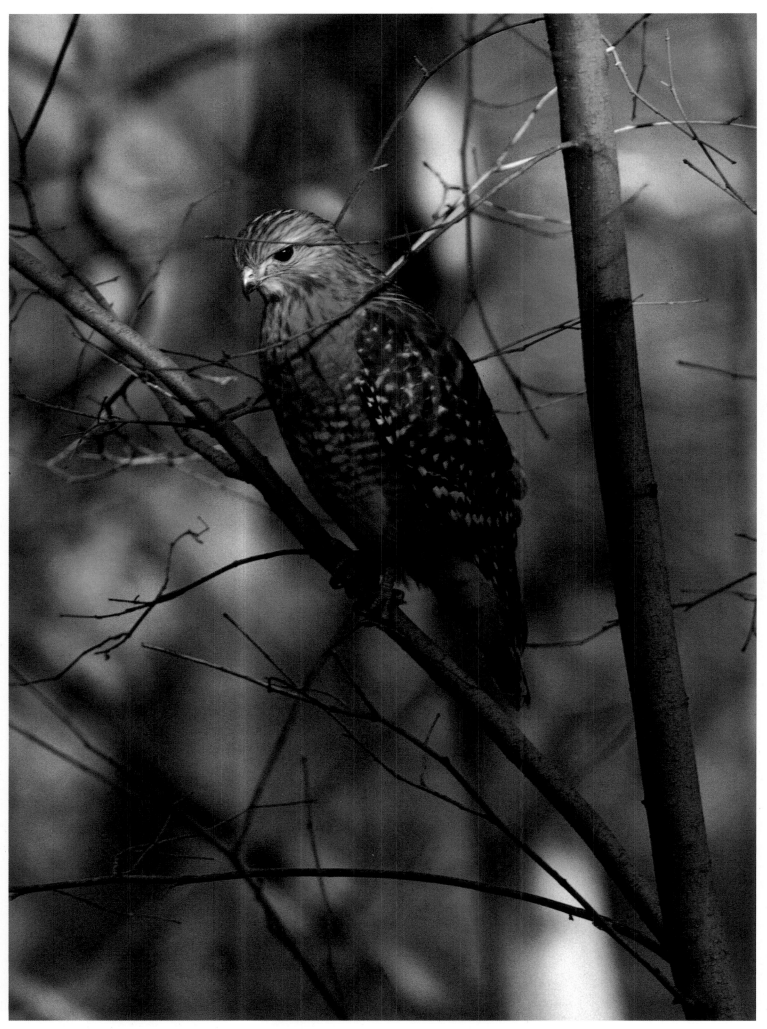

Red-shouldered hawk, keen-eyed resident of Virginia's woodlands FREDRICK D. ATWOOD

Dogwood leaves heralding autumn   DAVID MUENCH

" Then autumn comes, with all its pageantry, and the mountains and the valleys flame with gold and scarlet. As far as the eye can reach, a carpet of color stretches to the horizon. "

Virginius Dabney,
Virginius Dabney's Virginia

Spicebush swallowtail caterpillar showing the large eye-like markings that confuse and discourage predators   JOHN M. COFFMAN

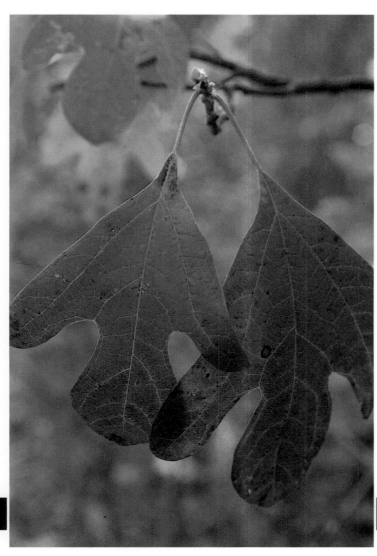

Flags of fall, sassafras leaves in
George Washington National Forest   CUB KAHN

Whitetail buck   ALAN D. BRIERE

66 *What he saw was fixed forever in his mind, the dull gray sky of the winter morning, the barren limbs of the sleeping trees, the virgin snow and the great deer which stood silent, immobile, and enduring through all of memory.* 99

Earl Hamner Jr.,
Spencer's Mountain

Maple leaves and winter's first snow   JOHN M. COFFMAN

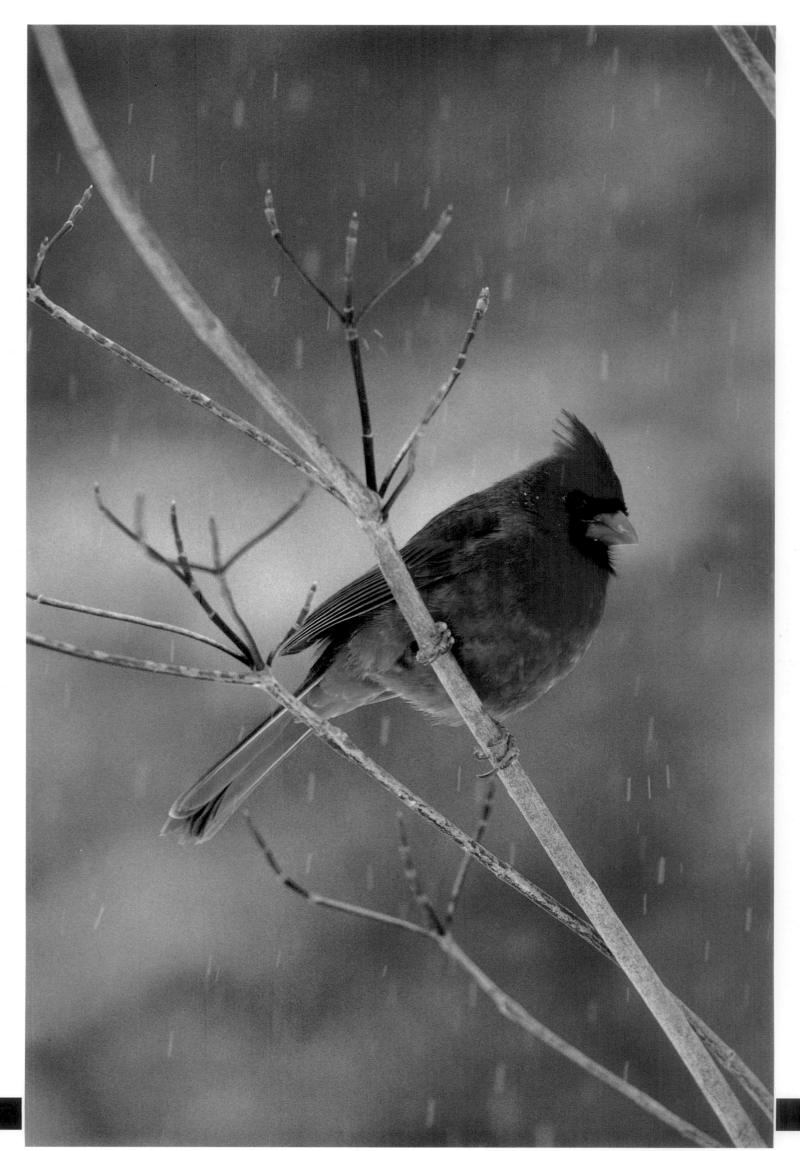

A cardinal, Virginia's state bird. surveying a snowfall   JOHN M. COFFMAN

Frosted leaves FRANK OBERLE/PHOTOGRAPHIC RESOURCES

Snow dusts an elderly oak in Chesapeake CECELIA JOLLEY/THE VIRGINIAN PILOT

" Virginia is a state for all seasons, but none is extreme. Each lasts only long enough to leave the wish that it had lasted a little longer. Even the winter has benign stretches, an old man dreaming by the fire of the days of his youth. "

Guy Friddell,
What Is It about Virginia?

Glassy Lake Drummond mirrors cypress trees in the Great Dismal Swamp

❝ The Great Dismal Swamp! The legendary land of untamed wild beauty astride the Virginia and North Carolina border— where dense forests sprout from spongy peat ground, threaded by canals and ditches, many grown over like green tunnels untouched by sunlight. ❞

Michael Frome,
Virginia

Gray squirrel   CUB KAHN

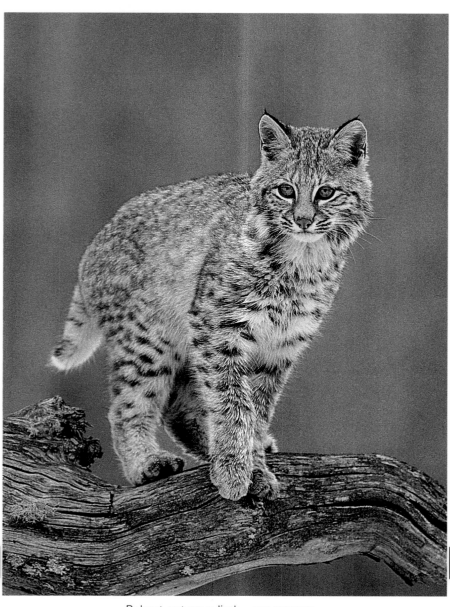

Bobcat out on a limb   TIM CHRISTIE

Girl Scouts, merry and meritorious   CATHERINE KARNOW

" *The great human law that in the end recognizes and rewards merit is everlasting and universal.* "

Booker T. Washington

Humble beginnings, the birthplace cabin of Booker T. Washington, near Hardy   DAVID MUENCH

Summiting on Mount Rogers, at 5,729 feet Virginia's highest point   FRED CRAMER

❝ *Even the mountains are moderate. They are old mountains, mellowed by time and the weather, grandfathers offering a knee to children. None is too steep to climb of a Sunday.* **❞**

Guy Friddell,
What Is It about Virginia?

Mealtime for pileated woodpeckers   JOHN M. COFFMAN

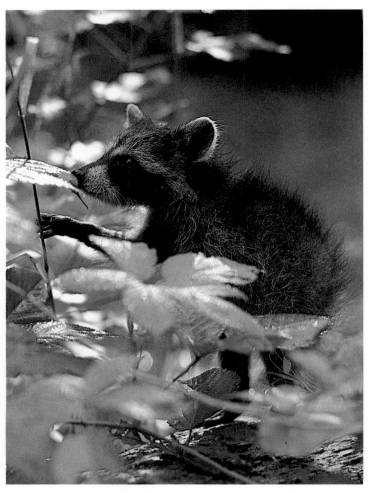

A curious three-month-old raccoon   LYNDA RICHARDSON

Natural Bridge, purchased in 1774 from King George III by Thomas Jefferson for less than $5   KENT & DONNA DANNEN

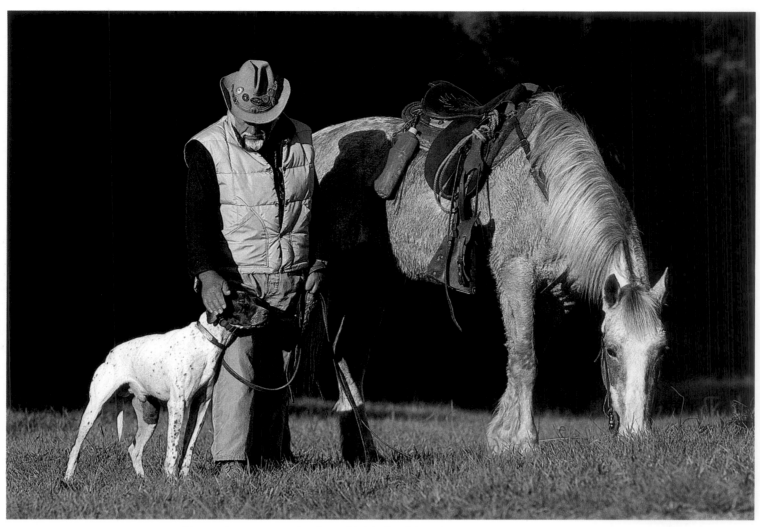

Dog trainer communicating with his English pointer   LYNDA RICHARDSON

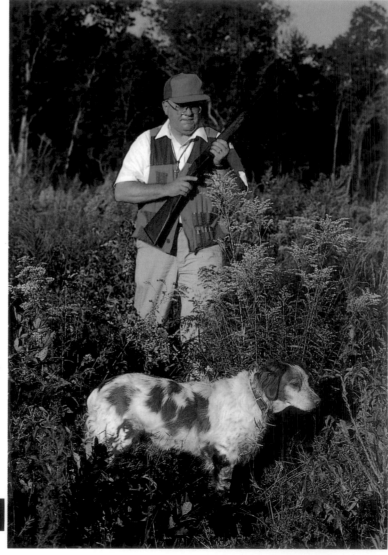

Walking up quail with a Brittany   LYNDA RICHARDSON

A pair of fillies near Charlottesville inspect the greener grass on the other side TAMARA VONINSKI/THE VIRGINIAN-PILOT

❝ *My native state is endeared to me by every tie which can attach the human heart.* **❞**

Thomas Jefferson,
Report of Virginia Assembly, 1809

Banks of the Potomac River in Westmoreland State Park   CARR CLIFTON

" *The passage of the Patowmac through the Blue ridge is perhaps one of the most stupendous scenes in nature....* "

Thomas Jefferson,
Writings

Spiderwort pushing through fallen leaves in Shenandoah National Park   WILLARD CLAY

Red fox   TIM CHRISTIE

Monarch butterfly on goldenrod   FRANK OBERLE / PHOTOGRAPHIC RESOURCES

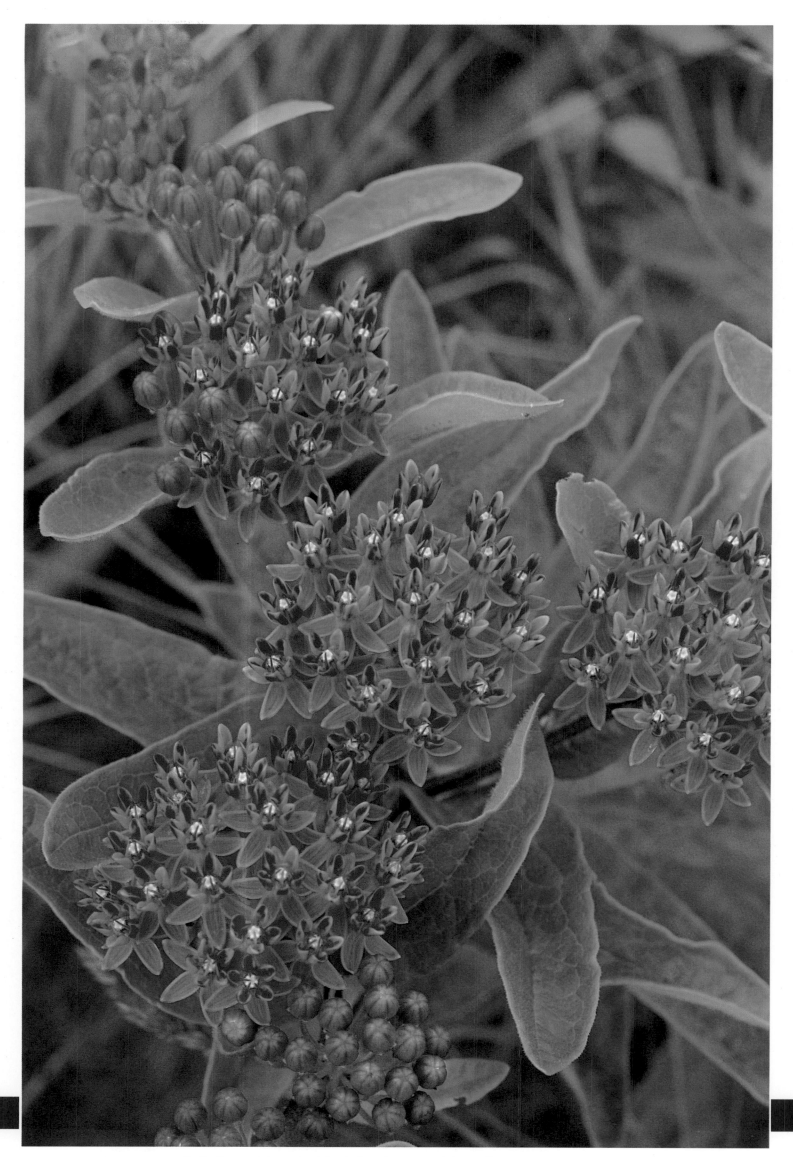

Butterflyweed, important food plant for monarch butterflies   ROBERT E. LYONS

Peaks of Otter along the Blue Ridge Parkway   TOM ALGIRE

Wood duck   JOE MACHUDSPETH

Mabry Mill, home of the "best cornmeal in the country,"
along the Blue Ridge Parkway near Meadows of Dan   JEFF GNASS

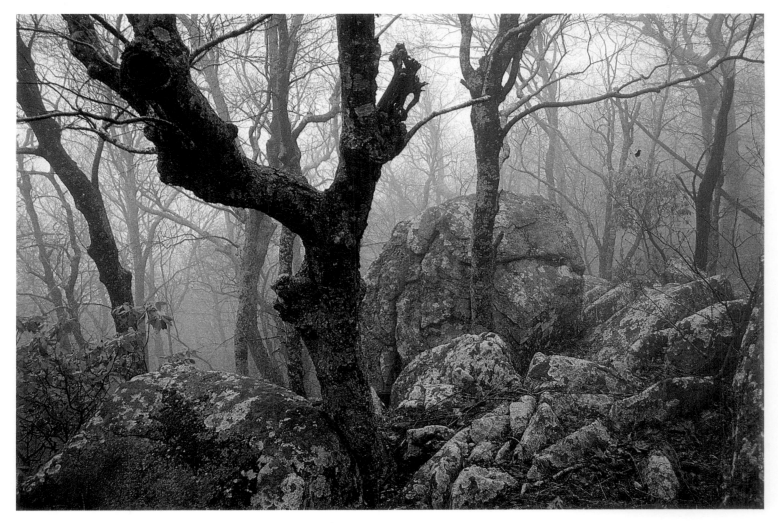

Clouds cloaking a Blue Ridge mountaintop   D.L. WINSTON

A downy woodpecker misses a beat
BILL LUBIC/PHOTOGRAPHIC RESOURCES

A veil of smoke from a controlled burn drapes the Great Dismal Swamp National Wildlife Refuge   STEVE EARLEY/THE VIRGINIAN-PILOT

Milkweed   CUB KAHN

“ The contour of the State offers every scenery—seacoast, tidewater, piedmont, mountains—as if to say, beguilingly, stay, it's all here, all that earth can afford. ”

Guy Friddell,
What Is It about Virginia?

Dawn along the shore of Virginia Beach CATHERINE KARNOW

In the sweet, undulating roll of [the name] Virginia, you can catch the soft folds of the Blue Ridge Mountains in the morning mist, the giddy, gaudy green Easter Egg hills billowing around Albermarle, the lazy James embracing Richmond, the dark green tobacco fields somnolent in the Southside sun, and the long, pale green combers rolling in white thunder on Virginia Beach.

Guy Friddell,
What Is It about Virginia?

Sunrise over Shenandoah Valley, Page County   CUB KAHN

they made it possible

Virginia on my Mind would have been impossible to produce without the creative and technical skills of more than forty professional photographers. These men and women succeeded in a difficult task—capturing the many moods and faces of the Old Dominion.

From the mountains to the sea, Virginia contains a breathtaking array of beautiful images, but transforming these images onto film requires more than just a camera. It takes an eye for composition, technical expertise, long hours of work,

and the sheer determination to obtain a memorable shot rather than a mere snapshot.

The photographers for *Virginia on my Mind* provided this extra skill and effort. They hiked, climbed, waited, and watched to get the best possible images from all parts of the state.

To all the excellent photographers who contributed to *Virginia on my Mind*, thank you.

The Globe Pequot Press

Photographers in *Virginia on My Mind*

Gene Ahrens
Tom Algire
Fredrick D. Atwood
Erwin & Peggy Bauer
Alan D. Briere
Tim Christie
Willard Clay
Carr Clifton
John M. Coffman
Fred Cramer
Kent & Donna Dannen
Derek Fell
Thomas R. Fletcher
William B. Folsom
James Frank
Raymond Gehman
Jeff Gnass
P. A. Gormas
Cub Kahn
Catherine Karnow
Zig Leszczynski/Animals Animals
Bill Lubic/Photographic Resources
Robert E. Lyons
Joe MacHudspeth
David Muench
Frank Oberle/Photographic Resources
Robert Perron
Lynda Richardson
Mae Scanlan

Scott T. Smith
Steve Solum
John Lewis Stage/The Image Bank
Connie Toops
Larry Ulrich
Glenn Van Nimwegen
D. L. Winston
Tim Wright

For *The Virginian-Pilot*:
Vicki Cronis
Steve Earley
D. Kevin Elliott
Mort Fryman
David B. Hollingsworth
Lawrence Jackson
Cecelia Jolley
Michael Kestner
Gary C. Knapp
Charlie Meads
Nhat Meyer
Motoya Nakamura
Christopher Reddick
Martin Smith-Rodden
Norm Shafer
Bill Tiernan
Tamara Voninski
Jim Walker

acknowledgments

Pages 8 and 24 quotes from *We Began at Jamestown*, by Guy Friddell. Richmond: The Dietz Press, 1968.

Pages 12, 14, 18, 30, 63, 84, 93, 104, 115, and 116 quotes from *What Is It about Virginia?* by Guy Friddell. Richmond: The Dietz Press, 1966.

Page 16 quote from *This Quiet Dust,* by William Styron. New York: Random House, 1982.

Page 20 quote from *Misty of Chincoteague*, by Marguerite Henry. Chicago: Rand McNally & Co., 1947.

Page 32 quote from *Bay Country,* by Tom Horton. Baltimore: Johns Hopkins University Press, 1987.

Pages 42 and 90 quotes from *Spencer's Mountain*, by Earl Hamner, Jr. New York: Dial Press, 1961.

Pages 45, 70, and 74 quotes from *Virginia Is a State of Mind,* by Virginia Moore. New York: E. P. Dutton & Co., 1942.

Page 46 quote from *Virginia Beautiful,* by Wallace Nutting. New York: Bonanza Books, 1935.

Page 48 quote from *Pilgrim at Tinker Creek,* by Annie Dillard. New York: Harper's Magazine Press, 1974.

Pages 52 and 98 quotes from *The Virginia Way,* by Guy Friddell. Offenburg, West Germany: Dr. Franz Burda, 1973.

Page 54 quote from "The Last Parade," by Douglas Southall Freeman, in *Virginia Reader: A Treasury of Writings*, ed. by Francis Coleman Rosenberger. New York: E. P. Dutton & Co., 1948.

Pages 76 and 96 quotes from *Virginia,* by Michael Frome. New York: Coward-McCann, 1966.

Page 78 quote from *Vein of Iron,* by Ellen Glasgow. Richmond: First and Merchants National Bank, 1963.

Page 88 quote from *Virginius Dabney's Virginia,* by Virginius Dabney. Chapel Hill, NC: Algonquin Books, 1986.

Page 100 quote from *Up from Slavery: An Autobiography,* by Booker T. Washington. New York: Doubleday & Co., 1963.

Page 108 quote from *Writings,* by Thomas Jefferson, ed. by Merrill D. Peterson. Literary Classics of the United States, 1984.

about Guy Friddell

One of Virginia's best-known and most respected writers, Guy Friddell wrote the introduction to *Virginia on my Mind.* A resident of Virginia for more than fifty years, Friddell is a columnist for *The Virginian-Pilot* and the *Ledger-Star* in Norfolk. His work also appears in the *Richmond News Leader.* Friddell has written nine books, including six about Virginia. One of his books, *What is it about Virginia?*, received a commendation from the Virginia General Assembly, and his most recent book, *Hello, Hampton Roads,* received a first-place award from Virginia printers. Friddell and his wife live in Norfolk.

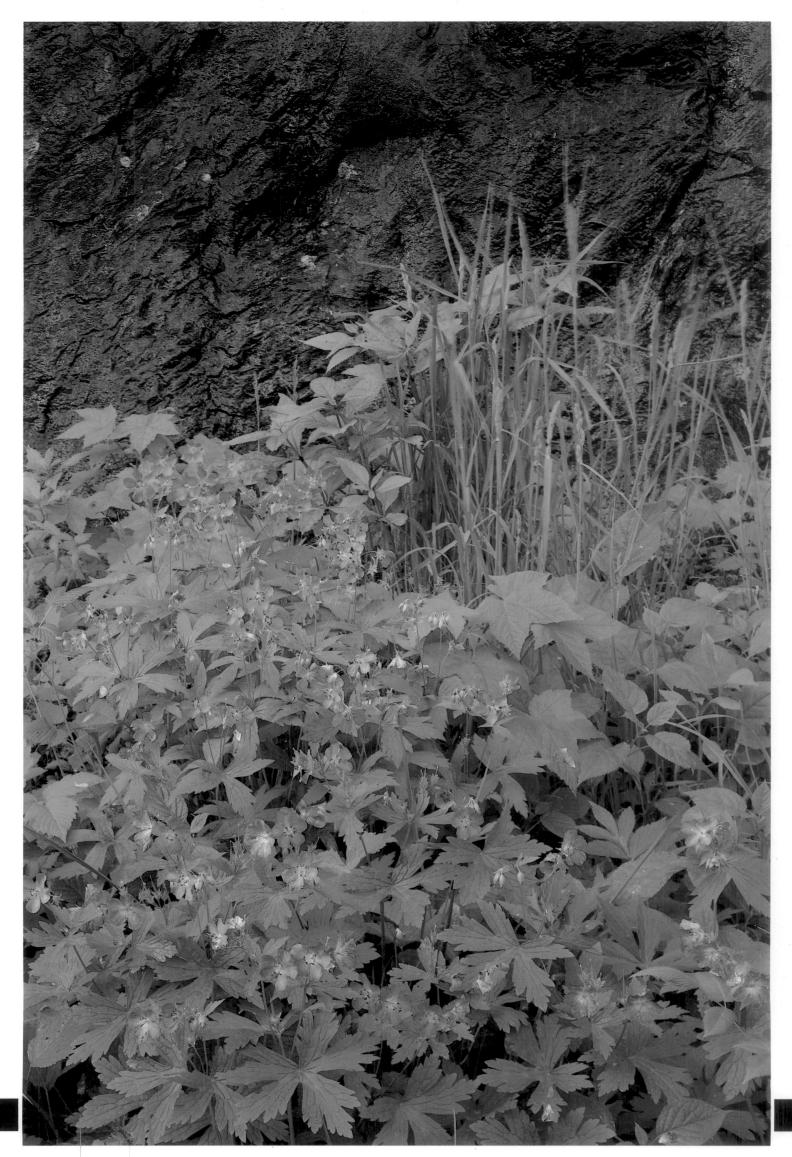

Wild geraniums in Shenandoah National Park   WILLARD CLAY